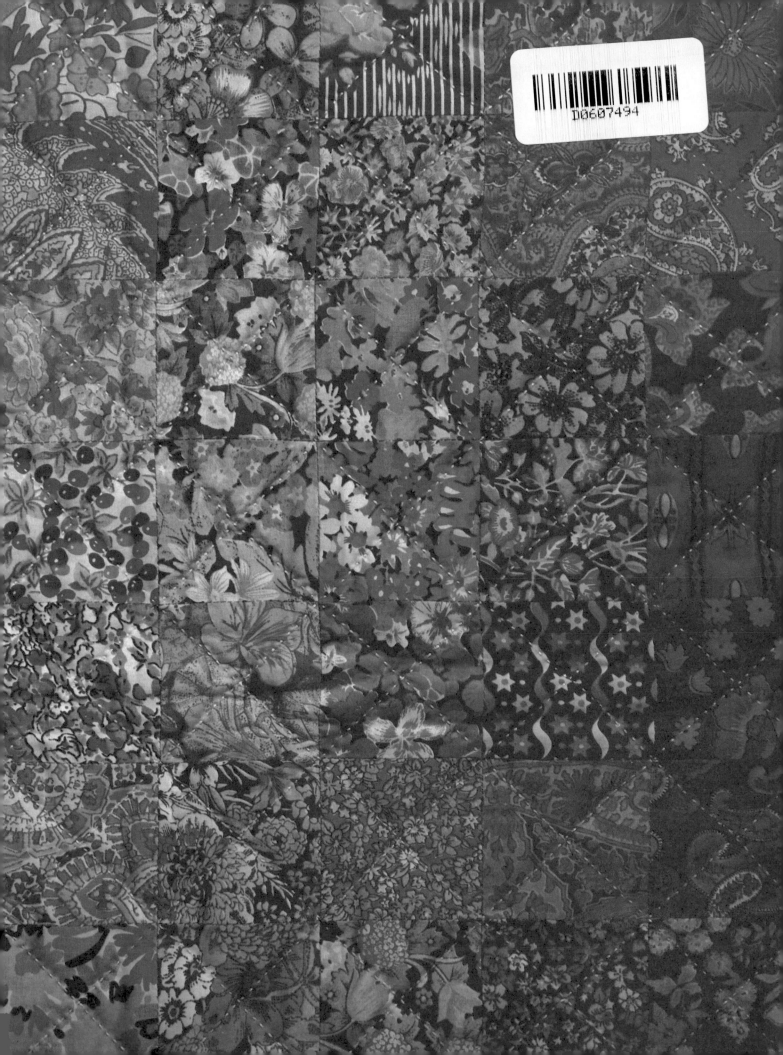

PATCHWORK

HELEN FAIRFIELD

CONTENTS

NOTES FOR AMERICAN READERS

Both the American and English methods for piecing patchwork are described in this book. Throughout the text the American term (where it differs from the British one) is given in square brackets.

First published 1980 by
Octopus Books Limited
59 Grosvenor Street
London W1

© 1980 Octopus Books Limited
Reprinted 1984

ISBN 0 7064 1344 X

Printed in Hong Kong

INTRODUCTION

Patchwork is the art of making pleasing mosaic patterns by cutting and sewing together scraps of material of different colours. There are two basic types of patchwork. *Pieced* work is the building up of pattern by seaming together shapes cut out of contrasting colours of cloth, while *patched* or *applied* work is used to achieve designs by applying cut-out shapes of one colour onto a contrasting background. While these techniques are commonly used separately they are often combined.

History

Patched or applied work must go back in history as far as the first woven garments. When a garment wore out in one place but was still serviceable, some practical genius produced the first patch. Pieced work probably predates weaving. Until very recently Eskimo women manufactured handsome outer garments of furs of different colours, piecing them together to form simple patterns. It would be surprising if Stone-age people had not done the same.

SURVIVING EXAMPLES
Because of the perishable nature of the materials employed and the wear to which they were subjected, very little patchwork has survived from ancient times. A funeral tent canopy was found in the tomb of Queen Esi-mem-Kev of Egypt who lived in about 980 BC. This was made of gazelle hide, with dyed shapes of scarabs, serpents, lotus flowers and other traditional motifs applied to a plain ground.

No clothing or hangings have survived from ancient Assyria, but glazed ceramic murals found at Khorsabad show kings dressed in clothing which could well have been patchwork, the patches being decorated with embroidery.

It is very possible that Joseph's coat of many colours, as described in the Bible, was made from patchwork.

In India, a votive hanging of rectangular pieces of silk and damask of different colours, and a bag made up of triangular and square patches of silk were discovered in the caves of the Thousand Buddhas and are believed to be at least 1200 years old.

Tradition has it that the Crusaders brought both kinds of patchwork back to Europe with them. Appliqué was certainly used on horse trappings and banners in place of, or combined with, embroidery, and some illustrations indicate that pieced work was also widely used.

A painting from a 13th century Spanish manuscript in the Escorial Library, *The Story of Count Garcia and the Devout Knight* by Alfonso the Wise, shows a knight clad in a surcoat, and his horse in cloth trappings, which echo the armorial bearings on his shield. These could have been made in the same way as the 'Streak of Lightning' or 'Snake Fence' pattern common in 19th century America.

A 15th century German miniature now in Munich shows horse trappings which are unmistakably pieced work, while the earliest literary confirmation comes from France – the 13th century *La Lei del Desire* – a book of poems which describes 'a bed of which the quilt was of a check-board pattern of two sorts of silk cloth, well made and rich'.

There are examples of applied work for clothing and house furnishings from the 15th century on, but it was not until fine cottons imported from the East became readily available in the 17th and 18th centuries that pieced work became common. Curiously, the earliest English pieced work to survive, the Levens Hall covers, and the earliest American quilt extant were made within a few years of each other. The Saltonstall quilt can be dated to between 1701 and 1704 by the newspapers used as patterns and left in the quilt, and, according to family tradition, the Levens Hall covers from Cumberland were made in 1708.

THE PATCHWORK QUILT
Improvements in weaving techniques made the Jacquard woven cloths more widely available, and the importing and subsequent domestic development of printing on fabric made applied work on clothes and household articles less necessary and less fashionable. From the middle of the 17th century the history of patchwork is almost exclusively the history of the patchwork quilt.

Blankets, as we know them, were not available until the 19th century. Bed coverings were either down-filled featherbeds, which served as both mattress and cover, or quilts which were two layers of cloth with wadding [batting] between, stitched together in patterns. Some of these quilts were white, or had tops of solid colour, but many had decorative tops made up by piecing together coloured scraps of material left over from dressmaking.

Above: This mural was painted on a wall of the Palazzo Pubblico, Siena, in 1329. It shows a man wearing a patchwork coat which is echoed in the trappings of his horse.
Opposite: This lovely example of crazy patchwork was made in 1884. It is worked in silk, velvet and satin, and decorated with a variety of embroidery stitches.

COLONIAL AMERICA

Patchwork has always been a woman's craft. Until comparatively recently it was generally considered unnecessary and undesirable to educate the daughters of the family beyond the rudiments of the three Rs. Instead, their education was centred on homemaking – on feeding the family, nursing them and clothing them. Even in wealthy homes in Europe this was a circumscribed existence; in colonial America it was also frugal and exhausting.

A young American girl hoped for a husband who was kind and a good provider. While waiting for him to turn up she helped her mother and from her learned homemaking skills. During such leisure as she had, she pieced and patched quilt tops. It was

expected that by the time she got engaged and these quilts were 'put in' to a frame with backing and wadding [batting] to be quilted, that they would number 12. The 13th would be made and quilted between the engagement and the wedding. Once married, she would have little time for piecing quilt tops.

The young man, for his part, looked for a sensible girl who would be thrifty and hard working. A wife was expected to make her own clothing and bedding. In areas remote from civilization she might be expected to spin, dye and weave the cloth as well. Cloth which she had made herself from the raw wool or flax would be precious and no scrap would be wasted. Printed cottons from England would be rare and even more valuable.

AMERICAN QUILTS

Some of the earliest quilts to be made in the American colonies had a homespun back with a top of plain colour in imported linsey-woolsey (a material with a linen or cotton warp and a wool weft) quilted together, sometimes with a carded wool wadding [batting] between the layers. Others had a medallion pattern using two or more colours of linsey-woolsey, a centre motif with multiple borders and decorated corners. With their long, straight seams these would be simple to put together. From them evolved the block quilts which are still with us. The pattern which decorated the 17th century quilt is repeated many times in miniature on the 19th or 20th century quilt. Each block of the latter quilt is easily worked in the hand and then all the blocks are joined together, probably with dividing bands, before quilting.

AMISH DESIGNS

The deeply puritanical Amish people continued this medallion tradition long after it had fallen out of fashion with other Americans. Their religion forbade them any form of outward show, or decoration for decoration's sake, so the Amish, who shared a love of vibrant colour with their less rigid Pennsylvania Dutch cousins, continued to make their medallion patterns in vivid combinations of unlikely colours. Many who know that the Amish dress sombrely in blacks, browns and greys are surprised that they should possess such hues, but they used vivid fabrics to line their clothes so that home-spun and home-dyed colours – bright oranges and greens, purples, blues and particularly reds – were ready on hand to combine with the dark colours to make their distinctive quilts.

PRINTED FABRICS IN PATCHWORK

Whenever they were available, English and American housewives made use of the printed materials which were first imported from India and later manufactured in England. (Wealthy women, like the makers of the Saltonstall quilt, used silk scraps.) Eventually, after the Revolution, printed fabrics were manufactured in America. Some old quilts can be dated to within a few years by the prints used to make them.

EARLY BLOCK TECHNIQUES

The makers of the first block quilts did not have templates to guide them. They designed their patterns by taking a square of paper the size required for the block and folding it again and again until they arrived at the pattern they wanted. A 'four block' pattern would be folded in half and in half again and then cut into four. The resulting quarters would be further subdivided horizontally, vertically, or diagonally as required.

The blocks thus achieved were given distinctive names. Names based on the Bible were common – 'Golgotha', 'Crowned Cross' and 'Hosanna'; political slogans were recorded –'Free Trade' and '54–40 or Fight'; but domestic titles such as 'Sister's Choice', 'Swing in the Corner' and 'Grandmother's Fan' predominated. Some blocks bear the same name all over the United States but others, which may have evolved separately in quite different places, may have several names. For instance one block is variously known as 'Bear's Paw', 'Duck's Foot in the Mud' and 'Hand of Friendship'. Some names have been corrupted with time – a simple swastika pattern, then popular as a good luck symbol, is called 'Fly Foot' instead of 'Fylfot'.

Above: A 19th century American children's menagerie quilt, worked in cottons.
Top: This quilt, known as 'Orange Baskets', is a good example of combined piecing and patching; the flowers and fruit were applied to the background after the basket had been pieced and sewn onto the backing.
Opposite: This mid-19th century American quilt is an example of the 'Rose of Sharon' design.

DIAMOND SHAPES

Not all pieced work was based on the block. Elaborate quilts were made by building up patterns with diamonds. The 'Star of Bethlehem' quilt starts with eight diamonds making an eight-pointed star, and continues out from that, either to make a whole quilt or to make large blocks. Diamonds are also used to make hexagons, joined together to make 'Tumbling Blocks' or 'Baby Blocks' quilts.

More elaborate patterns are made by combining the diamonds for the eight-pointed star with squares, and the diamonds for the six-pointed star with hexagons. The hexagon, by itself, is traditionally used to make a rosette quilt, but many elaborate patterns can be worked out by judicious use of colour.

CRAZY PATCHWORK

When times were really hard, precious scraps were used as economically as possible by applying them to a background and turning them into 'crazy patchwork'. Curiously, this became fashionable in Victorian times and crazy patchwork covers of silks and velvets, embroidered elaborately, were displayed on divans in fashionable drawing rooms.

LOG CABIN PATCHWORK

Another type of patchwork is the 'Log Cabin' design, which is built up with strips of fabric laid around a central [center] square and sewn down onto a backing block. This patchwork does not use wadding [batting] and is self-quilting in its original form, as will be explained in a later chapter. Although the Log Cabin patchwork requires more sewing than most other blocks, since there is no need to quilt the finished article, it is probably as quick to finish as the more conventional methods.

APPLIED PATCHWORK

Of course, not all quilts were pieced. In the early days, motifs from Indian and English chintzes were cut out and applied by stitching onto plain backgrounds. Later, shapes of flowers, leaves, birds, insects and animals were cut out to apply onto plain backgrounds to build up designs. Sometimes there would be a combination of pieced and patched work in one block, as in the 'Garden Basket' design. This 'patched' tradition has continued, alternating in fashion from place to place and from time to time, with pieced patchwork, until the present day.

OTHER METHODS

Missionaries took the art of quilt making to Hawaii where it was transformed. The Hawaiians used their traditional patterns and applied large, intricate patches in one vivid colour onto white, and then proceeded to quilt around the patches in lines echoing the outlines of the leaves.

Three other types of patchwork are worthy of note. The Seminole Indians in Florida decorate clothing with a very effective method. They sew bright colours together in strips of equal width and then cut them at right angles to the joins [joining]. These new strips are then joined up with the colours staggered, the resulting band being inserted into the garment at an angle.

The San Blas Indians of Panama lay three or more colours of cotton one on top of the other, baste them together, and then achieve a pattern by cutting away and hemming back to a line first the top layer and then the second, leaving the lowest layer as an accent.

The final method is known as 'Cathedral Window' and involves careful folding of background material into squares, which are then joined together, using a second colour as accent. This is a very decorative method which is 'self quilting'.

CHANGING ATTITUDES TO HANDCRAFTS

The Industrial Revolution in the latter part of the 19th century

radically changed patchwork. It provided a wealth of inexpensive printed cottons, which meant that women did not have to rely on their 'patch bags' to save up material for a quilt, but could go out and buy what they needed. The invention of the sewing machine made unnecessary the meticulous skills of fine sewing which were lost within two generations. Wool blankets were available for sale at a reasonable cost and were lighter and often warmer than the cotton-filled quilts. Possibly more important, especially in America and Canada, houses were better heated by furnaces which fed radiators in bedrooms and it was unnecessary to pile the beds so heavily in order to keep warm.

At the same time there was a revolution in the status of women. Free education was available to both girls and boys and it became possible for girls to look outside the domestic circle for employment. Except in a few households handwork came to be considered 'old-fashioned' and patchwork quilts were tucked away in trunks in attics, if not actually thrown out. Only in a few remote country districts did the tradition of making and using patchwork quilts persist.

THE MODERN REVIVAL

In the last quarter century, however, there has been a revival of interest. Labour-saving equipment in our homes provides a leisure which our great-grandmothers would have found unbelievable, while the variety of fabrics is greater than ever before. Patchwork is one of the very few crafts where the beginner need not be daunted by the necessity to acquire advanced skills before being able to express his or her desire to be creative. All that is needed is an ability to measure, mark and cut out accurately, and to execute neatly such elementary stitches as running stitch, stab stitch, oversewing [overcasting] and slip stitch. Having mastered these simple skills, the world of patchwork is open to you.

MATERIALS AND EQUIPMENT

Suitable fabrics

The ideal material for patchwork is a firmly woven, opaque, pure cotton material which has been pre-shrunk and proved to be colourfast. Anyone visiting the fabric halls of today's department stores will quickly realize that such material is becoming more and more difficult to obtain. Cottons are mixed with synthetic fibres which add strength and prevent creasing but make it difficult to achieve the crisp folds necessary in either pieced or applied patchwork. Plain materials are frequently so fine they show a shadow of the seam allowance through a patch unless backed by another material.

Diligent search may discover the pure cotton ideal in suitable colours and patterns but excellent results can be achieved with other materials provided a few simple rules are kept in mind.

It is essential that fabrics which can all be cleaned by the same method be kept together, odd ones being put aside for use elsewhere. The rule of thumb is: cottons with cottons, silks with silks, etc.

To achieve a harmonious effect and to ensure equal wear, fabrics should be of the same weight throughout. Do not, for instance, mix voile with heavy poplin. If you propose using some newly purchased material with material which has been used but is still serviceable, it is advisable to wash the new cloth before using it to guard against uneven shrinkage.

Knitted material is difficult to handle and should only be used with other knits, never with woven material. It is possible to stop jersey pulling out of shape by ironing on shapes of felted fibre interfacing but this does tend to make a stiff patch which has a limited use.

Velvets, fine corduroys and needlecords make attractive patchwork, but do remember that the apparent colour of velvet can be changed quite remarkably if the pile is not kept running the same way in all the patches. This effect can, of course, be used to advantage, but a good deal of careful thought is required at the design stage if the finished article is to be successful.

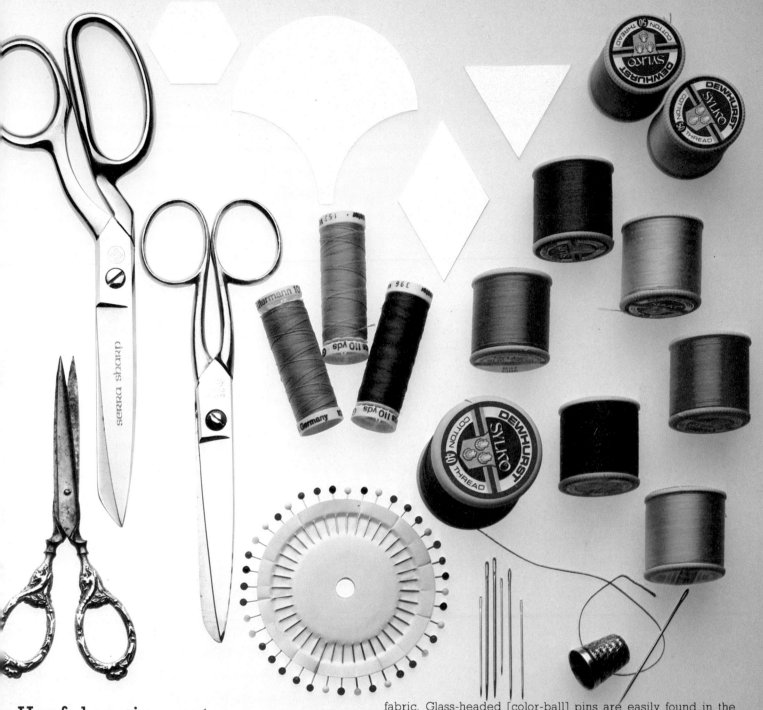

Useful equipment

Much of the equipment for patchwork will be found in any dressmaker's workbox.

There should be three pairs of scissors. A good, sharp pair of dressmaker's shears are essential for cutting the fabric, but should never be used for cutting paper as this will dull the blades, which should be of good steel to hold an edge. Left-handers will find it worthwhile to purchase a pair made for left-handed people.

Paper-cutting scissors should be sharp enough to cut crisply, and large enough to be handled comfortably.

A fine pair of embroidery scissors will make snipping off ends and clipping seam allowances for curves less of a chore.

Needles should be as fine as you can comfortably use, as tiny stitches are necessary. Whether you use Sharps, Betweens, Straws [Milliners] or even Crewels is a matter of personal choice, but the size should not be larger than an 8, and 9 or 10 would be better. (The larger the number, the smaller the needle.)

Buy the finest pins you can find as coarse ones may mark the fabric. Glass-headed [color-ball] pins are easily found in the workbox. When using delicate silks and satins use fine needles in place of pins, as they will not mark the fabric as much.

Use soft basting thread for basting the fabric to the paper patterns. For permanent sewing use fine cotton or synthetic thread in a colour which will be inconspicuous against the colour of the patch. Silk thread should be used for sewing silk or velvet.

A thimble is essential. Buy one which fits comfortably on the second finger of your right hand (if you are right handed). You may find that you will also need a tailor's topless thimble for the index finger of the other hand.

Each patchwork piece made by the English method should be pressed before joining it to the next, and each seam sewn by the American method must be pressed open or to one side, so you will need a good iron, a pressing cloth and an ironing board.

Should you intend to make quilts by the block method, and if you enjoy using a sewing machine, you will find that you will use a straight stitch machine a good deal. In some techniques a swing needle machine with decorative stitches would also be useful, but all patchwork can be done by hand.

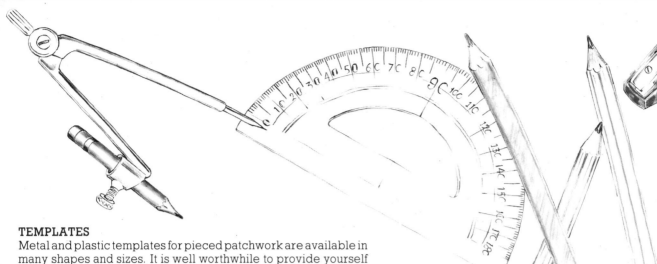

TEMPLATES

Metal and plastic templates for pieced patchwork are available in many shapes and sizes. It is well worthwhile to provide yourself with at least the smaller sizes in popular shapes as small templates are difficult to cut accurately out of card [cardboard] and wear badly in constant use. The sets which provide a metal template and a matching plastic window template are particularly useful. You may, however, find that the size of template you need is not available. Hexagons and the diamonds for six-pointed stars are easily manufactured by following the lines on isometric paper. Should isometric graph paper be difficult to obtain (it is sold by draughtsmen's suppliers) it is possible to make the templates you need if you have a ruler, compass(es), and protractor.

Templates should be cut, very accurately, out of stiff card [cardboard]. Fashion board is only barely strong enough for the purpose. You will need a sharp craft knife and a steel-edged ruler, as well as some sort of cutting board. The shape should be drawn first with a hard pencil and then cut very carefully. (A template only minutely out of shape will cause maddening problems throughout the making up of the article.)

The hexagon

To draw a hexagon, establish a radius equal to the length of the side of the desired figure and draw a circle. Place your compass point anywhere on the circumference of the circle and draw an arc, making sure that the opening of the compass is still equal to the radius of the circle. Move the point of the compass to the point where the arc crosses the circle and draw another arc. Continue around the circle. You will find that you have six equidistant points. Join these points with straight lines (**fig. 1**).

The six-pointed star

To obtain a diamond for a six-pointed star, draw another circle with the radius the length desired for the sides of the diamond. Draw a hexagon and join the two points A & B to their opposite points E & D. You will find you have two diamonds the size you require as well as corresponding equilateral triangles (**fig. 2**).

The eight-pointed star

Diamonds for an eight-pointed star are also easy. Draw a line A-B the length you want for the sides of the diamond. Using your protractor, draw a line at 45° to this line. Place your compass on point A and using radius A-B, bisect this line at C. Move the point of your compass to C and draw an arc. Bisect this with an arc made using B as your point. Join the points arrived at (**fig. 3**).

The pentagon

A pentagon is a somewhat more difficult figure but it can be achieved with a protractor. First draw a line a-b and mark on it the length of the side desired, A-B. Place your protractor on this line and draw a line from B at an angle of 72° to a-b. On this new line mark your length, B-C. From C draw another line at an angle of 72° and so on (**fig. 4**).

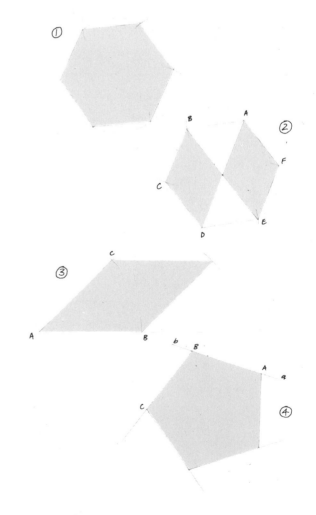

If you purchase commercial templates, the size of the shape is usually given as the length of one of its sides. For instance, a 2.5cm (1in) diamond, square or hexagon would have sides of that measurement.

Other shapes

Hexagons and diamonds are the most common templates used in patchwork, but others can be very useful when designing. The square and the triangle (which is formed by drawing a diagonal across the square from corner to corner) are often used, as is the octagon, which needs to be arranged with a square to make a pattern. These, and the long hexagon, sometimes called the 'Church Window', can be designed on square graph paper or by measurement.

The clamshell template is a mushroom shape which can be made up by drawing interlocking circles with a pencil and compasses.

For Cathedral Window patchwork you simply need a paper pattern of the basic square; while the only requirement for Log Cabin patchwork is the careful measurement and cutting of the width of the strips.

SPECIAL DESIGN PAPER

For designing you will need squared graph paper and isometric paper. The designs for many pieced articles can be worked out in miniature on isometric paper and then enlarged by counting sections on the paper. The shapes can then be traced onto stiff card [cardboard] and cut out to make templates.

Most isometric paper is stiff enough to be used as the actual patterns for pieced work (see English method page 15). The design can be drawn out full size, cut out and each piece used as a pattern paper with the miniature version remaining for reference. Once your design is cut out, it is a good idea to mount your miniature and the individual pieces in position by pinning onto a cloth-covered board. As you cover each piece, it is pinned back into place on the board. This guards against the loss of a vital piece of fabric, and it means that you can correct mistakes in colour and tone.

Designs based on squares and rectangles can be worked out on graph paper and then enlarged by using the squared paper sold for pattern design in dressmaking. This, however, is too flimsy to be used as pattern papers and it will be necessary to make up templates from card [cardboard] or plastic. If you have a favourite pattern which you use again and again, it may be worth while having it made up in light metal.

OTHER EQUIPMENT

You will need a selection of coloured pencils or felt-tipped pens for designing, and dark and light coloured fabric marking pencils for drawing around templates onto the fabric, in those instances where this is necessary.

Paper patterns can be made out of cartridge paper [art paper] but used envelopes, used writing paper or the pages of glossy magazines will do as well.

It is essential that all templates and pattern papers are cut accurately. Pieced patchwork is a jigsaw puzzle: if the pieces are cut clumsily they will not fit together and lie flat.

The other vital piece of equipment needed is a well filled scrap bag. Into this will go the remnants from dressmaking, that sample from the remnant counter which caught your eye, the remains left over from specially purchased patchwork material from another project. This 'scrap bag' may be a spare drawer, a box in a cupboard, or, for the dedicated patchworker, it may be a series of drawers or boxes with the material sorted by colour, by fibre and by weight. When starting a new project you may purchase a good deal of the material, but the accent which will set off the design is likely to be lurking in the scrap bag!

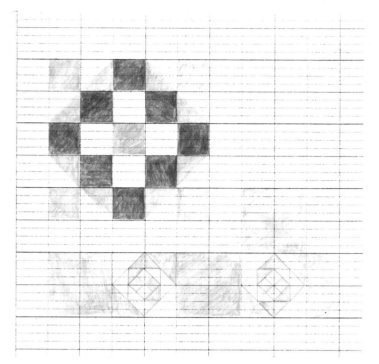

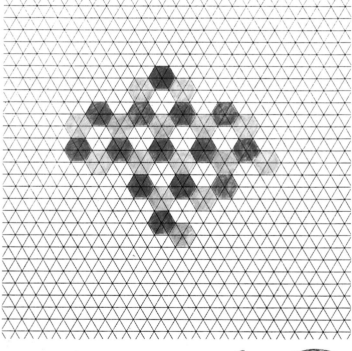

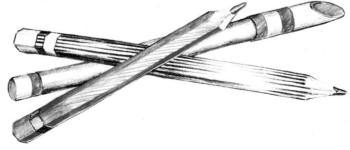

TECHNIQUES

Piecing is the method of joining together shapes of fabric to form a design. While in the past the term 'patchwork' generally referred to piecing, it also means the decoration of fabric by appliqué, so we must be explicit.

Methods of piecing

There are two methods of piecing patchwork.

In one, a paper pattern is required for each piece. The fabric is cut big enough to overlap the pattern and is basted to it securely. The paper is not removed until the patch has been securely attached to its neighbours. This method is traditional in England but is employed elsewhere where small and interlocking patches are required, or where it is essential that the finished work lies absolutely flat.

In the second method, the cloth is marked on the wrong side where it is to be sewn, using a pencil and a firm metal or card [cardboard] template, then cut out leaving an adequate seam allowance. The patches are next pinned together carefully to match up the pencilled lines, then joined by stitching along these lines. This is the method traditionally used in the United States and in several countries in Europe.

THE ENGLISH METHOD

Each method has its advantages. The English method is very accurate and produces a strong fabric. Ideally it is done by hand. After the seam allowances have been turned over the pattern papers and basted in place, the two patches are placed right sides facing and oversewn [overcast] together using tiny stitches and avoiding the pattern papers as much as possible. The patches can only be joined by machine by someone who commands great skill. Patches can either be machined together by oversewing [overcasting] the edges with a swing needle machine, or by basting the patches to a background material and sewing them down while joining them together with a decorative machine stitch. It is difficult to get satisfactory results by the first method, and the effect of the second method is attractive but quite different in character to the patchwork joined in the normal way.

THE AMERICAN METHOD

The American method is much quicker than the English when done by hand, and lends itself easily to machine sewing. Block designs made by building up straight-sided shapes such as triangles and rectangles are often put together in strips and then the strips are stitched together. This is very easily accomplished by machine when speed is important.

Some American blocks have patches with curved lines. It is preferable to sew these by hand as they are difficult to sew together accurately by machine, even when the patches are basted together along the seam lines first.

This hexagon patchwork quilt was made in England in the 1830s. It provides an interesting record of the wonderful variety of printed cottons being manufactured in England during this period. The traditional rosette motifs, picked out in white, harmonize with the floral fabrics used for the outer borders.

CHOOSING THE METHOD

Once both methods of piecing have been practised the one you will use in the future will be very much a matter of personal preference and suitability for the design to be worked. The smaller the pattern, the more likely it is that you will use the English method because of the need for accuracy in joining the many small pieces. You may also find that the English method is preferable for designs with curved lines. If the design is large and has straight-sided patches, or if you want to complete the work as quickly as possible, you may prefer to use the American method. Even on interlocking patterns, the American method will probably find favour if the design is large enough and the patches have straight sides.

The two methods can best be explored by making two sample pieces, a place mat by the English method, and a potholder by the American. Although they will be quite different in shape they may be made of the same materials – good quality, dressweight cottons. For the first you will need at least two colours, for the second, four. The colours should go well together but display a degree of contrast in tone.

You will need basting thread, sewing thread of a suitable colour, and a supply of thin wadding [batting] or foam sheeting. Dacron or terylene [polyester] wadding [batting] is suitable, but any soft material which can be packed tightly will do.

Project in English patchwork

To make a simple place mat by the English method take a sheet of isometric graph paper and draw on it a rosette of seven hexagons with sides about 5cm (2in) long (**fig. 1**). Cut

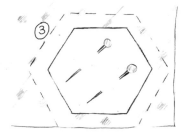

these out very carefully with your paper-cutting scissors. If you have no isometric paper available, take a 3.5cm (1½in) commercial metal template and cut seven exact hexagons out of cartridge paper [art paper] by holding the template in one hand and cutting exactly against each edge with your scissors (**fig. 2**). Do not try to

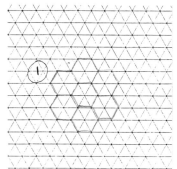

trace around the template with a pencil and then cut out as the margin of error is doubled by doing so.
Choose two colours of your dressweight cotton material.

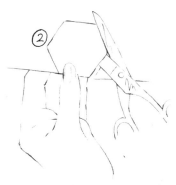

Place a paper hexagon on the wrong side of the first fabric with one edge exactly on the grain line and pin securely in place with two pins (**fig. 3**), making sure that you have left room to cut seam allowances of at least 6mm (¼in) all around.
Place the other six hexagon patterns on the wrong side of the second, contrasting piece of cotton fabric and pin in place (**fig. 4**), making sure the grain lines are matched up and that there is room between the patterns for two seam allowances. Now cut out carefully. It is better to err on the side of extra width than to make the seam allowance too narrow.

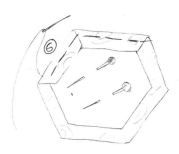

Take the first patch and fold one seam allowance over to the back of the patch, making sure that the fold lies tight against the edge of the paper. Thread a needle with basting thread, take a back stitch in the seam allowance to secure the thread, and then take stab stitches through all three thicknesses – seam allowance, paper and the front of the patch to hold the fabric firmly in place (**fig. 5**).

When you get to the first corner, fold the next side down and secure the corner with a stitch (**fig. 6**).

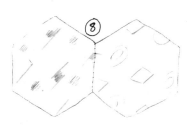

Continue until all six sides are finished and fasten off with a backstitch.
Baste the seam allowances firmly into place on each of the other six hexagons. Remove the pins.
Now take the odd coloured centre hexagon and one of the six of the other colour. Check that the grain lines match up, then fold them over, right side to right side, edges touching. Thread your needle with a sewing thread of a suitable colour, no more than 40cm (16in) long or it will tend to knot. Start off by taking two or three back stitches through the seam allowance near the corner where you mean to start. Run the thread through to the corner and then sew the two edges together with a succession of tiny oversewing [overcasting] stitches (**fig. 7**).

Ideally you should pick up one or two threads from the material of each patch without touching the paper patterns. Work the whole line and cast off with back stitches through the seam allowance.
Open the patches out flat and examine the right side. The stitches should be firm and almost invisible (**fig. 8**).
Join the other five hexagons to the centre in the same way, ensuring that the grain of the patches match up. When the rosette is complete, (**fig. 9**),

remove the basting thread from the centre patch and extract the paper. If you have not stitched into the edges of the paper it can be used again.

The floppy centre will allow you to fold the two adjacent hexagons onto each other so that their right sides are facing and you can match up the

edges. Oversew [overcast] the adjoining edges, making sure that no gap is left between this line of oversewing [overcasting] and the lines of sewing connecting the two hexagons to the centre hexagon (**fig. 10**). Continue until all six hexagons are joined to each other around the centre patch.

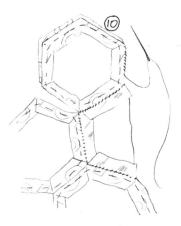

Make a second rosette to match the first, possibly reversing the colours. Remove all the basting threads and all the paper shapes. Cut out a matching hexagonal shape of thin foam rubber sheeting or synthetic wadding [batting], measuring 6mm (¼in) less all round. Lay on the wrong side of the second rosette, and slip stitch lightly along the edges to attach. Turn over, and lay the first rosette in place, wrong side up. Oversew [overcast] all the edges neatly together, leaving a pocket large enough to turn the place mat right side out. Finish off on the right side as neatly as possible (**fig. 11**).

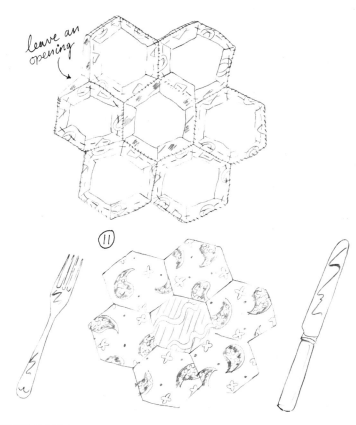

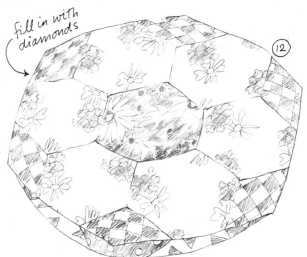

HEXAGON AND DIAMOND COMBINATION

A useful variation on the rosette place mat is a hexagonal shape where the 'Vs' between the hexagons are filled in with diamonds (**fig. 12**). Instead of making two similar pieced shapes, a back and a front, this shape may be backed with one hexagonal piece of plain fabric.

HOW TO USE DIAMOND SHAPES

When we use diamonds to fill in the corners of the rosette place mat we find ourselves presented with a new problem. The acute angles in the diamond can be difficult to manage. The diamond templates are cut either by using isometric paper or by cutting against a metal template. The paper patterns are pinned onto the fabric, leaving seam allowances, and cut out. Be sure not to skimp seam allowances at the points Starting at a blunt angle, fold the fabric over to the back and baste into position (**fig. 13**).

To turn the sharp point two methods are possible. When using light material which folds easily, fold the point of the material down, making sure you don't turn over any of the paper inside the fold (**fig. 14**). Now make a second fold, along the line of the second side of the diamond, and stitch into place (**fig. 15**).

With thicker materials or materials which do not fold easily, do not fold the point over, but leave a tab at the point. When the piece is stitched to other pieces this is carefully kept out of the way (**fig. 16**).

Making a six-pointed star

There will be little difficulty in sewing diamonds to hexagons, but you may wish sometime to sew diamonds into a six-pointed star. The logical way to set about this would seem to be to stitch one diamond to another around in a circle, but this is almost certain to present you with an unwanted gap in the middle.

To avoid this, join up two sets of three diamonds. These are then joined by a single oversewn [overcast] seam with no weakness in the centre (**fig. 17**).

USING WINDOW TEMPLATES

Although patchwork is stronger and holds its shape better when the grain lines on all the patches run the same way, there are times when it is desirable to cut the material across the grain in order to make a feature of the patterns printed on the fabric. The commercial 'window' templates make it possible to pick out the part of the patterned material you want to use, and it is simple enough to make your own window out of a postcard by cutting out the shape of your template, and then cutting again around a 6mm (¼in) seam allowance.

Experiment with your window by trying it on different parts of your fabric and then select patterns which appeal to you. When you have made your choice, lay the window template on the right side of the material, carefully centering it on the motif you wish to use. Draw around the outside of the template and cut out carefully. Now position the paper pattern taken from the pattern template on the back of the patch and pin in place, making sure that all seam allowances are equal. Baste up in the usual way, checking the front of the patch as you sew.

Make further patches in the same way and join them together to make a pattern.

Some fabrics, especially floral stripes, lend themselves particularly well to designing with the use of a window template or templates. Sometimes it is possible to build up the design for a whole cushion [pillow] using only one piece of fabric by carefully selecting portions of it. It is surprising how a simple twist of the template will alter a pattern and the effect it gives when made up.

VARIATIONS ON THE DIAMOND TEMPLATE

A popular use of the diamond template based on the hexagon is the Baby's Block or Tumbling Block pattern (**fig. 1**). In this, three diamonds are joined together to make a hexagon.

These hexagons are then joined into an all-over pattern which gives the impression of a series of cubes in perspective (**fig. 2**). Although a variety of fabrics may be used, it is necessary to keep the pattern of tones constant or the illusion is lost. If you start with the 'top' medium in tone, the 'left' diamond light and the 'right' diamond dark, this must be maintained in all the blocks.

Another variation possible is the combination of diamond shapes with one central hexagon, and a gradation of colours from light to dark (**fig. 3**).

The eight-pointed star is another favourite template and is the basis for the Star of Bethlehem pattern. This is a little more tricky than the six-pointed star as the points are even sharper, but with care should present no more difficulties. The star can fill the whole shape, or the corners can be filled with squares. Squares by themselves are rarely very interesting, but they are useful in combination with octagons (**fig. 4**).

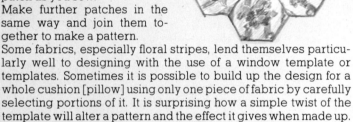

PIECING WITH CURVED SHAPES

So far, we have dealt only with straight line blocks. Occasionally it is necessary to piece a pattern with a curved line, although the simplest method is to apply the curved motif. For instance, if you wish to make a panel in pieced work depicting a rising sun, you would join the rays of the sun in the usual way (**fig. 1**), but the sun would present problems.

First, cover the 'sun' template in the usual way, but take small tucks in the curve (**fig. 2**).

Now, lay the completed rays, face up, next to the sun, and ladder stitch the two together with stitches as small as you can make them (**fig. 3**).

Draw the two curves together as tightly as you can as you go along.

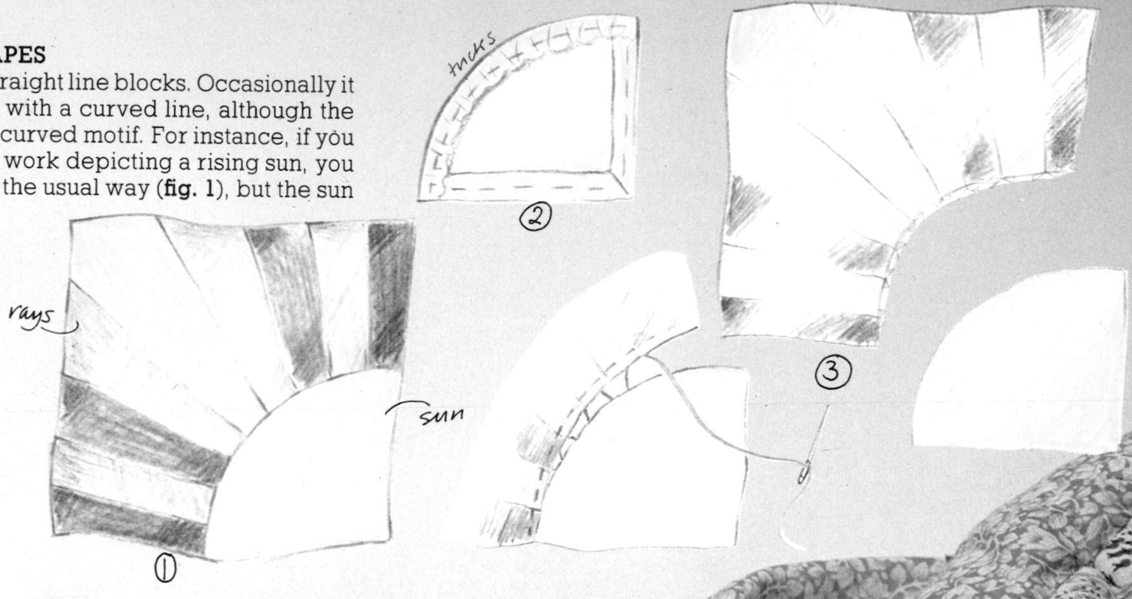

rays

sun

tucks

①

②

③

Project in American pieced work

The American method of piecing patchwork dispenses with pattern papers. It works very well for all patterns based on the rectangle and triangle.

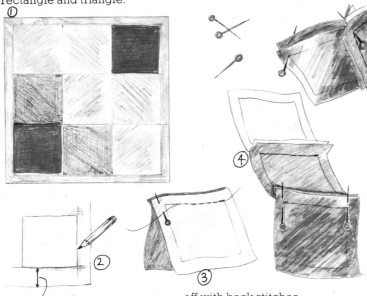

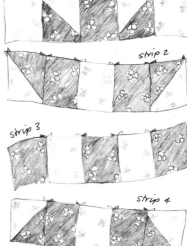

To make a typical American pieced block, as the basis for a potholder, cut a 7.5cm (3in) square out of firm card [cardboard], or use a commercial square template. Choose four colours of cotton material. It will help if you draw out your pattern (**fig. 1**).

Making sure that one edge of your template is precisely on the grain of the material, and leaving a minimum of 6mm ($\frac{1}{4}$in) allowance available all around, draw around the template with a hard pencil (**fig. 2**). You will need two squares of three colours and three of the fourth. Cut out, leaving ample seam allowances.

Arrange your patches in the order you require them.

Lay the top patch in your main colour face down on the right side of a patch of your second colour. Using pins, match up the corners of the pencilled squares. Take a needle threaded with a suitable colour and, starting at one corner, take a back stitch or two and then follow the pencilled line to the other corner with tiny running stitches, making sure that you sew through the pencilled lines on both patches (**fig. 3**). Finish off with back stitches.

Now join a patch of the third colour (**fig. 4**). Make a second strip, using patches of colour four, one and two.

Make a third strip, using three, four and one. Press with a hot iron and a damp cloth.

Now join strip one to strip two (**fig. 5**), and strip two to strip three to make a square (**fig. 6**), using pins to match the seams. Either make a similar square for the back, or cut a square from one material. Lay your patchwork square, carefully pressed so that it is quite flat, face to face with the second square and sew around it with small, firm running stitches, leaving an opening in the centre of one side.

Clip the corners to reduce bulk, turn through to the right side, and stuff lightly with wadding [batting], before stitching up the opening. As it is essential that the wadding [batting] remain in position during use, the potholder must be quilted, either along the lines of sewing or inside the squares.

It is essential that the running stitches should be even and close together or the stuffing will come through. Close the opening with inconspicuous oversewing [overcasting].

THE BASIC QUILT BLOCK

This potholder illustrates the method in its simplest form, but is the basis for all American quilt block patterns based upon the square and the triangle. Let us, for instance, take a traditional pattern such as 'Sister's Choice' (**fig. 7**).

To make a block 37.5cm (15in) square (which can be used for a cushion or as one block for a quilt) you will need one template 7.5cm (3in.) square and a triangle template which is half of that.

Choose two colours of material contrasting in tone and mark and cut out eight light-coloured squares and nine dark ones.

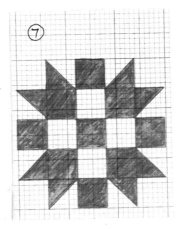

Mark and cut out eight light and eight dark triangles. Sew the light and dark triangles together along the diagonal line to form eight squares.

Now join five strips (**fig. 8**), five squares in each strip.

Press and sew together, matching up the seams exactly as for the potholder. This is a method easily adapted for the machine.

make 8 squares

strip 1

strip 2

strip 3

strip 4

strip 5

Patchwork Quilts

METHODS OF JOINING QUILTS

One of the commonest methods of joining blocks for a quilt is with 'lattice bands'. These are strips of material of uniform width which separate each block from its neighbours. There may or may not be a different colour used where the strips intersect, or there may be a special block pieced to look after this aspect of the design.

Take a length of material the colour you have decided will best set one block off from another and cut strips of the required width plus turnings. Cut these strips the length of the side of the block and join them to the sides of the blocks (**fig. 1**) by hand or machine, arranging the blocks into rows of the required number.

Now either take one long strip of the dividing fabric and sew it along the top and the bottom of the first strip of blocks, or join up strips, incorporating contrasting blocks where they will meet the dividing bands in the first strip of blocks (**fig. 2**).

If you are using contrasting blocks, great care must be taken to see that these meet the corners of the pieced blocks accurately. This will mean careful measuring of the strip and connecting block, and very accurate stitching.

Blocks may also be set on the diagonal of the quilt, especially when each alternate block is blank, or a variation of the main block. This will mean that three plain templates are needed, (**fig. 3**), one for the main block, one for half and one for a quarter block.

DESIGNING THE BORDER

However you set the quilt, it will need a border. This may be an extension of the lattice bands, a plain bound edge, or a specially designed border. Quilts designed to have a deep overhang should have the corners squared off so that the quilt will not touch the floor (**fig. 4**). The overhang is frequently treated as a border, with motifs echoing the main blocks in shape and colour.

BACKING AND LINING THE QUILT

Patchwork quilts must have a backing and traditionally also have a lining of wadding [batting] for warmth. This used to be wool or cotton but synthetic fibres available today are lighter, hold their shape better, and are more easily cleaned.

The backing should be a lightweight fabric of the same fibre content as that used for the top. For a large quilt you will need to seam together several widths. There is no rule as to where these seams should lie, but their placing should be thought out as a design, rather than left to haphazard arrangement. Seams should be pressed open crisply [sharply] or to one side.

If the quilt is to be bound, the backing should be cut slightly larger all around than the top, and then trimmed to fit after quilting. If the backing is to serve as binding it should be cut at least 2.5cm (1in) larger all around than the top and the wadding [batting].

Press the top and the backing, and then lay the backing out on the floor or other large space, seam side up. It is a good idea to tape the backing to the floor to hold it in place. Now lay the wadding [batting] on top of the backing and smooth it out. Finally, lay on the pieced top, right side up, and smooth into place.

Start from the centre and baste all thicknesses together with long stitches. First work to mid-top, then mid-bottom and mid-sides to form a cross; then work diagonal lines to the corners. Use a very long thread to make it unnecessary to join threads in the middle of a row of basting.

Once this is done, start in the centre again and baste in concentric rectangles, about 25cm (10in) apart, until the final row holds the edges of the three layers together.

It is essential that the backing remains flat when basting. Be sure that all layers remain even; it is worth while spending time on this process as it saves time later.

USING A QUILTING FRAME

Ideally the quilt should now be set into a quilting frame, but these may not be easily available to the beginner. Quilting can be done in a round wooden quilting hoop about 58cm (23in) in diameter. This is like an embroidery hoop but is deeper and therefore stronger. It does not need so much effort to set up, nor does it take so much space as a frame. The hoop may be used on a stand or propped against a table or chair. The basted layers should be pulled taut in the hoop. If there are distortions they will be quilted in and be there for ever. Now quilting can begin: use a fine needle and cotton thread about 40cm (16in) long. Sewing is done with a single strand. Start with a knot on the top surface, run the needle through the middle for about 2.5cm (1in), and start sewing with a back stitch. The knot is cut off later and the thread disappears between the layers. When the thread is finished, take a back stitch and then run the needle between the layers and through to the top. The stitch used is a short running stitch, worked one stitch at a time through all three thicknesses. You will need a thimble.

Quilting may be done by machine, the preparation of the layers being the same. Excess material on each side of the working area should be rolled up out of the way, and the hands used to smooth the work being fed under the needle, taking great care that wrinkles are not sewn in where stitched lines cross. Always work from the centre of the piece outward.

The design of quilting is as complicated as the design of patchwork and we lack the space to go into it here. Basically, the quilting designs should echo the lines of the block and, of course, spaces may be left unquilted for effect.

Marking is done by pencil against a ruler or the edge of a curved template on the top of the piece. The pencil lines will disappear at the first washing.

When the whole area has been quilted the quilt can be bound. As previously suggested, the backing material can be brought forward and folded over the front and basted and then hemmed into place. (To attach a separate binding, see method page 25.)

Other kinds of patchwork

We have dealt at length with pieced work but there are other types of patchwork. The most important of these is applied work.

CRAZY PATCHWORK

The simplest applied work is crazy patchwork. Work in this technique can vary from a haphazard hotch-potch to a carefully thought out abstract collage, depending upon the materials to hand and the skill of the patchworker. Modern crazy patchwork requires a backing, a filling or batting, and a selection of materials. It can be worked equally well by hand or machine.

Decide the size of your finished article – a cushion [pillow] is a good project to start with – and cut the preshrunk backing to size. On this place a layer of polyester wadding [batting] and baste it in position (**fig. 1**). Working from one corner, select the first piece of fabric and

pin it in place, face up (**fig. 2**). Take the next fabric and lay it, face down, edge to edge with your first fabric. Pin and sew through all the layers. Fold to the right side and pin in position (**figs. 3a, 3b**). Continue in this fashion until your background is completely covered.

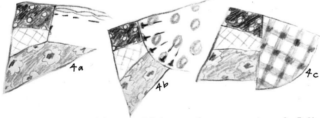

There are some problems which may be encountered. A light fabric laid over a dark one must have turnings wide enough to prevent any shadow of the dark material showing through. Right angles can present difficulties (**fig. 4a**). The space can be covered by a curve (**fig. 4b**). This is pressed over and pinned into position to be finished off with embroidery later.

A straight line can be sewn across it, but this is wasteful and will necessitate trimming away some of the fabric already applied (**fig. 4c**).

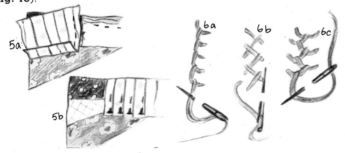

Probably the best way out of the difficulty is to lay one side of the new piece in the usual way (**fig. 5a**) and sew it down, folding under the second edge and pinning it into position to be held with embroidery later (**fig. 5b**).

Crazy patchwork is traditionally finished off with embroidery which also serves to quilt the piece. Machine embroidery will do this very well, but hand embroidery, which can be bolder, is often more effective as a feature of the design. The stitches most often used are the blanket stitch variations (**fig. 6a**), herringbone (**fig. 6b**), and feather stitch (**fig. 6c**), but any stitch which seems suitable can be used.

The traditional block pattern, 'Grandmother's Fan', is a development of this technique. An example of this pattern is on page 31. The rays of the fan are applied to the block which must be of an attractive material as a portion of it will remain uncovered, and sewn into place in the same way as the patches for crazy patchwork are applied. Care must be taken to ensure that the tapers on all the rays are the same. The centre of the fan and the outline are applied by folding the edges under and pinning them in place. Unlike crazy patchwork, these pieces are generally hemmed down inconspicuously instead of being embroidered.

CLAMSHELL PATCHWORK

Clamshell patchwork combines the paper pattern piecing with the applied technique. Cut a very accurate clamshell pattern out of a piece of light card (a postcard is ideal) and pin it to the right side of your fabric (**fig. 7**). Cut out leaving seam allowances and keep it pinned securely in place.

Now fold the fabric to the wrong side, away from the card [cardboard] shape. Take tiny running stitches to anchor the gathered turning to the main shape, checking constantly that the folded edge follows the top edge of the template (**fig. 8a**). Do not attempt to fold over the seam allowance on the inside curves, but it is worthwhile to follow these shapes with marking stitches. Remove the card [cardboard]. The front of your patch should look like **fig. 8b**.

When assembling the clamshells it is useful to stretch a length of elastic between two pins on a cloth-covered board (**fig. 9**). Pin your first row of patches to the board, with the elastic giving you a straight line as a guide.

The second row is put in place by fitting the tops of the clamshells into the basted guidelines on the first row. Baste the rows together as you go along, moving the elastic down as you start each new row to ensure that your lines remain straight.

Clamshells may be hemmed to the row above to make a fabric, or placed on a background of lining and wadding [batting] and hemmed together and quilted at the same time, depending upon the use to which you are putting them. They can also be arranged in various ways to make different patterns (**figs. 10a, 10b**).

LOG CABIN DESIGNS

Another favourite applied patchwork is Log Cabin which can be done either by hand or machine. There are three methods of making the basic square.

For the first, cut a backing square the size of the finished block plus turnings. Find the centre by folding diagonally, then baste the diagonals so that you may continue to use them as guides (**fig. 11a**). Cut a 3.8cm (1½in) centre square from a fabric which will give an accent of colour to the finished block. Cut a number of 2.5cm (1in) wide strips following the grain of material from fabric in progressive shades of two colours, say pale to deep pink and mid to navy blue.

Pin and baste the accent square to the centre of the backing patch, lining up the corners with the diagonal lines (**fig. 11b**).

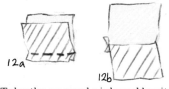

With your lightest pink, lay a strip over the centre patch, face down, matching the edge with one edge of the square (**fig. 12a**). Cut off excess, and stitch down, by hand or machine, 6mm (¼in) from the edge. Turn over and press (**fig. 12b**).

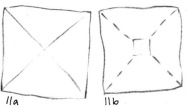

Take the second pink and lay it at right angles to the first (**fig. 13a**). Cut off excess and stitch in position (**fig. 13b**).
All corners must be right angles and all seam allowances exactly 6mm (¼in). Obviously, great care must be taken in all measurements.

Preparing a grid

A quicker way to ensure accuracy is to mark out the backing piece before you start, using graph paper, dressmaker's carbon and a tracing wheel. Stitch the accent square to the centre (**figs. 14a, 14b**). The grid is then used as your guide for machining the strips in place. This means that cutting the strips need not be so meticulously accurate as the finish does not depend on this.

Quick machine method

An even quicker machine method dispenses with the backing altogether. Cut very accurate 2.5cm (1in) strips. Sew the first one to the centre square (**fig. 15a**), right sides facing, stitching 6mm (¼in) from the edge. Open out and press (**fig. 15b**).
Lay the second strip at right angles and sew at 6mm (¼in) from the edge. Continue until the centre square is surrounded (**fig. 15c**).
Now cease to measure from the outside edge. Using a quilting guide if necessary, sew 13mm (½in) from the first machined line, on the back of the patch. This makes a truly accurate square much easier to achieve (**figs. 16a, 16b**).

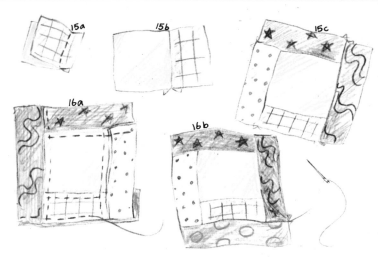

There are a number of variations on the Log Cabin block, as illustrated, but there is even more variety in the ways they may be put together to make a pattern for cushions [pillows], or quilts.

APPLIED BLOCK TECHNIQUE

The true applied block is not so frequently found today, but in the last century this type of patchwork reached a peak of popularity, and examples of the time show a high standard of design and technique. One favourite pattern was the 'Prairie Flower' (**fig. 17**). This elaborate quilt was made up of large blocks and smaller joining blocks, connected by latticed bands of the background material.

The main blocks were made up as shown. Individual templates were made for the three shapes in the flower, the three in the bud, and one for the leaves (**fig. 18**). The stems were made by cutting strips of bias material, folding the edges over, and sewing one side down on the fold line with running stitches. The second side was then hemmed down. (**figs. 19a, 19b**).

The pieces for leaves were prepared in the same way as the clamshell patches, by pinning the pattern to the right side of the material, and folding and basting the edges over to the back, but the flower shapes were more difficult as the inside angles had to be snipped before turning them over (**fig. 20**).

The shapes were pinned in place, and then hemmed down as inconspicuously as possible.

Modern appliqué quilts tend to be Alphabet Quilts, Menagerie Quilts, or Picture Quilts.

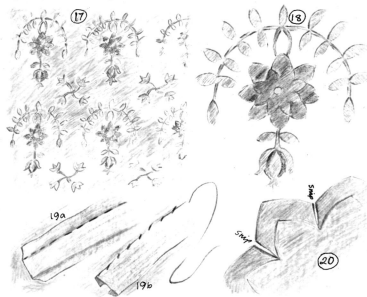

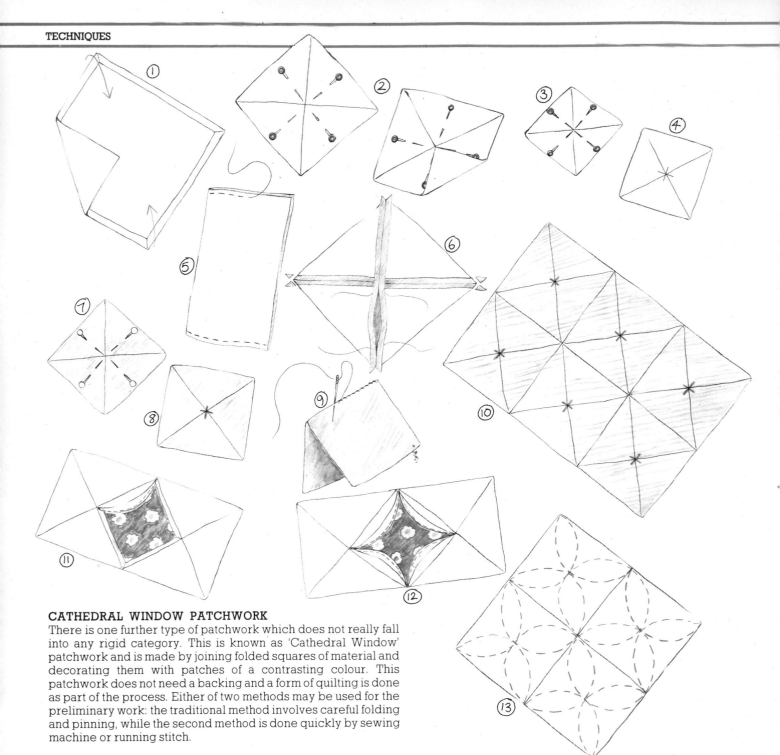

CATHEDRAL WINDOW PATCHWORK

There is one further type of patchwork which does not really fall into any rigid category. This is known as 'Cathedral Window' patchwork and is made by joining folded squares of material and decorating them with patches of a contrasting colour. This patchwork does not need a backing and a form of quilting is done as part of the process. Either of two methods may be used for the preliminary work: the traditional method involves careful folding and pinning, while the second method is done quickly by sewing machine or running stitch.

First method

Cut the required number of 15cm (6in) squares (**fig. 1**). Fold 3mm ($\frac{1}{8}$in) seam allowances round the square and press firmly. Fold the corners to the centre and pin (**fig. 2**). Fold these corners to the centre (**fig. 3**) and pin. The first pins should lie in the gaps between the folds. Stitch a decorative cross to hold the centre firm (**fig. 4**). Remove the pins.

Second method

Fold your square in half, right sides inside, and stitch, by hand or by machine, 3mm ($\frac{1}{8}$in) from the two ends (**fig. 5**). Press the seams open, and fold the materials so that it is possible to sew the remaining sides together, leaving space open to turn through to the right side. Clip excess fabric off the corners before turning through (**fig. 6**). Fold the corners of this square to the centre as in the first method, and pin in place (**fig. 7**). Secure the centre with a decorative stitch (**fig. 8**).

The procedure is now the same, whichever method you have chosen for the preliminary work. Place two squares together, right sides facing, and oversew one edge securely from corner to corner (**fig. 9**). Open out. Continue to join the patches until you have sufficient for your purpose (**fig. 10**). Do try to see that no spaces are left at corners.

Now cut 2.5cm (1in) squares from a decorative fabric. One of these is placed over the seam between two blocks, positioned carefully, and pinned in place.

Thread a needle with a thread matching the background material, curl back one edge over the edge of the 2.5cm (1in) square, and stitch in place through all thicknesses of material (**fig. 11**). Continue around the square until all four edges are complete (**fig. 12**). You will find that a quilted effect has appeared on the back. The finished article should look as though quilted with a design of intersecting circles (**fig. 13**).

Finishing Patchwork

BINDING EDGES AND MITRING CORNERS

Many projects in this book require binding around the edges and mitring at the corners to achieve a good, neat finish. The following method combines binding and mitring in one process, and can be used as a standard procedure wherever binding is recommended.

To make the binding

Choose a suitable fabric to make binding strips. Mark and cut out strips on the straight grain of the fabric. (Use bias strips only if you are binding a curve.) Cut the strips four times the finished width required for a single binding, and six times the finished width for a double binding.

Join the strips with diagonal seams into one continuous length.

Join enough to fit around the edges of the work, plus about 15cm (6in) extra.

For a double binding fold and press the binding in half, wrong side inside.

If the binding is very long, loop it up loosely and secure with a pin. Release a little at a time as you work.

To attach the binding

The binding is first attached to the *right* side of the work.

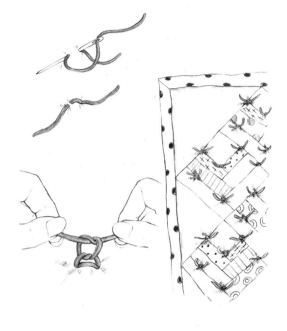

Start at the middle point of one of the edges of the patchwork. Pin the binding on through all the layers, matching the raw edges together. Leave about 10cm (4in) of binding hanging free, and pin along to the first corner. To begin the mitre, fold the binding up and over to make a 90° angle and pinch it to mark a diagonal crease (**fig. 1**). Insert a pin along the crease. Baste the binding to the patchwork through all the layers, up to the inner corner of the crease, them machine stitch 6mm ($\frac{1}{4}$in) in from the edge. Fasten off threads (**fig. 2**).

To continue along the next edge, do the second stage of the mitre. Fold the binding up along the existing crease, and down again to lie along the next edge of the patchwork (**fig. 3**). Pin, baste and machine the binding along the edge until the next corner. Repeat the same procedure as above until the starting point is reached. Join the two ends of the binding with a diagonal seam. Remove basting threads, and fasten all ends off securely. Clip away any excess wadding [batting] and backing around the edges.

Turn the work to the *wrong* side, and fold the binding over to meet the line of machine stitches. Pin in place, and fold corners as shown (**figs. 4–5**) for

a neat mitre. Hem the edges of the binding and the diagonal seams of the mitred corners to finish (**fig. 5**).

KNOTTING

Quilts are quilted partly to hold the wadding [batting] in place and partly for decoration. Modern wadding [batting] holds its position much more successfully than the natural fibres which used to be employed. It is possible, therefore, only to tie the layers together in places. It is a useful method when the layers of a quilt are so thick that quilting is difficult. However, knotting is not as durable as quilting.

It is advisable to make the knots on the seams of the

patchwork and not in the centre of patches where they may pull through the fabric and leave a hole.

Use a strong thread of natural fibre (synthetic thread will not hold the knot). Make a stitch through all the layers of the quilt, leaving a tail of thread. Then make a back stitch over the first, and bring the needle out on the same side of the fabric. Tie the two thread ends in a tight reef knot. Finally, trim the ends to about 1cm ($\frac{3}{8}$in), or, alternatively, thread them back through the layers.

French knots, coloured beads or buttons can be used in conjunction with knots to give a more decorative appearance.

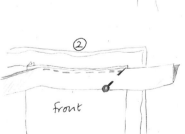

front

①

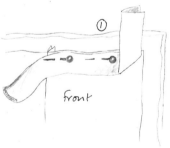

front

②

front

③

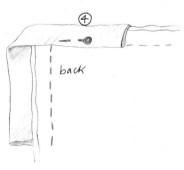

back

④

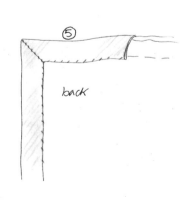

back

⑤

DESIGN

The possibilities for design in patchwork are almost unlimited. Source material can be anything from Roman pavements to Cubist paintings and so long as you have a ruler, pencil and graph paper you can easily work out your own variations to suit the requirements of your current project.

WORKING TO SCALE

One important factor to be kept in mind is scale. While it is quite acceptable to make a quilt of hexagons with 2.5cm (1in) sides if you have the leisure and the patience to make such an undertaking feasible, the quilt will look 'busy' unless the hexagons are grouped into units to make up a design which is pleasing to the eye because it relates to the size of the quilt. On the other hand, a needlecase made up of 5cm (2in) hexagons would seem crude and clumsy unless these hexagons were exquisitely decorated with embroidery.

As a general rule, unless you are deliberately working in miniature, making doll dresses or furnishings for a doll's house, any template with sides less than 13mm ($\frac{1}{2}$in) is too small to be practical, while huge hexagons with sides 7.5cm (3in) or over should be kept for such things as garden cushions [pillows].

Block patterns are another matter. There is no reason why you should not enlarge a block to make a whole quilt in the 17th century fashion. Such a design might be used to great effect for a duvet cover where a more complicated pattern would be lost.

USING COLOUR SUCCESSFULLY

Colour is even more vital. Your first consideration when planning a project is the colours you will use, and how they will blend with their surroundings. A cushion [pillow] or a quilt may be a work of art in itself, but if its colours clash with those of the room in which it is to be, it is a disaster. Don't rush to make yourself a bag in the lovely shades of green you found on a remnant counter if all you wear is blue. And think twice about making yourself a padded patchwork jacket in bright colours if those extra pounds you wish you hadn't got just won't go away.

Most of us remember learning about the colour wheel at school and it's a good idea to refresh our memories. A safe rule for a beginner is to use shades of one colour from one side of the wheel with an accent of the colour directly opposite – oranges with a touch of blue, lavenders with gold. Be very careful when using colours which are neighbours – cerise with orange is unlikely to work successfully for even the very clever manipulator of colour.

It can be very tempting to play safe and stick to those colour coordinated prints which provide half a dozen variations of pattern printed on white with the same dye. At first glance these seem ideal but the finished article is generally so bland as to be deathly dull unless a touch of another colour has been introduced as an accent to bring the whole arrangement to life.

COLOUR IN HOME FURNISHINGS

Cushions [pillows] should be designed for the room in which they will be used. They may echo the colour schemes of the room, but unless they introduce some contrast the overall effect may very well be drab. In a colour scheme which is itself low-key the cushion [pillow] may be the accent. A room which is predominantly cream and brown could have cushions [pillows] in bright oranges and gold.

There may be a time when new curtains have been introduced and a need is felt for their colour to be echoed somewhere else in the room. With plain fabric this is not too difficult, but a floral chintz may present problems. In this case, careful use of the window template can pick out areas of colour in the curtains and build them up into a design which uses the colour but changes the pattern. Alternatively, patches of the fabric could be combined with plain fabrics in neutral tones.

When making a set of cushions [pillows], or the blocks for a quilt, remember that it is possible to use the same pattern and the same fabrics, but to get completely different effects by changing the sequence in which they are used.

Opposite below: Effective use of red and green against a white background.
Opposite above: Log Cabin quilt worked in harmonious dress cottons.
Below: Mid-19th century, Irish pieced and appliquéd quilt.

PATCHWORK QUILT DESIGNS

Right: 'School Houses' was a popular pattern in the second half of the 19th century, usually being worked in red cottons, although other colours were used. The design is thought to have originated in New Jersey, but it was popular throughout the New England States.

Below right: This simple patchwork, made in Ireland in the last century, is remarkably effective. It shows that the simplest combinations of form and colour should not be despised.

Below left: This is a 20th century example of Hawaiian patchwork, using the design of Queen Kapiolani's fan in red and white cotton. The quilting follows the outline of the appliqué in rows about 2.5cm (1in) apart. The motifs used in Hawaiian quilts are symbolic and recur in different combinations on different quilts.

Opposite, above right: This simple Pennsylvanian Amish quilt is made of fine wool. The simple design, called 'Bars', is elaborated by delicate quilting, diamond patterns being used on the bars and feather quilting on the outer border.

Opposite below: This mosaic appliqué quilt is made up of a series of borders of piecework surrounding a centre block, where printed motifs have been cut out and appliquéd to a plain background, thus making the fragments of printed material go a very long way.

Opposite, above left: This patchwork is based on the eight-pointed star and the pattern is called 'Starburst' or 'Star of Bethlehem', depending on where it was made.

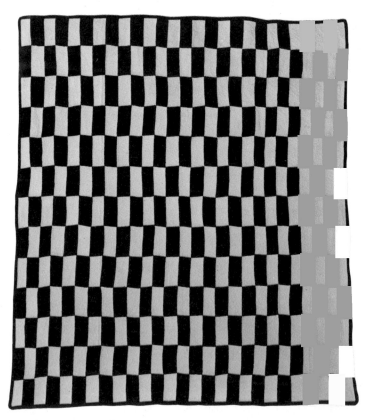

Opposite: The 'Baltimore Bride' quilt is an applied quilt made in the mid-19th century. It is suggested that the blocks were worked by friends of the bride and put together as a wedding gift. So many similar quilts have survived that it is possible that blocks were drawn out professionally or even that materials were supplied in kit form.

Above: This quilt is based on the eight-pointed star, but the motif has been enlarged by means of pieced and appliquéd borders to make it up to a double bed size. One border is less successful than the others as the maker has obviously been short of material and had to patch lengths together to make it up.

Right: This quilt is called 'Fanny's Fan' and is a variation of the 'Grandmother's Fan' pattern discussed on page 22. It was pieced from silks, ribbons and brocades, applied to a dull black satin and enriched with embroidery. It was probably intended as a sofa 'throw' instead of as a bed quilt, but was never used; it remained in the 'hope chest' of a spinster prevented by religious differences from marrying the man of her choice.

PAPER FOLD TECHNIQUES

Traditionally, American quilt blocks were designed by folding paper, rather than by using templates or by careful measurement. A square of paper the size of the finished block could be folded in half, the resulting rectangle being turned and folded in half again. This produced the simple 'four-patch' block which could be elaborated by further folding of the four patches (top row).

A block folded in three each way was called either a three-, or, more commonly, a nine-patch block. Again the basic blocks were elaborated by further folds (third and fourth rows).

Of course, the folds could be more numerous. A great many traditional American blocks are based on the five-patch fold (second row).

These blocks were given local descriptive or commemorative names, which might vary from one part of the country to another.

Quilts were generally made up of blocks of one pattern, often with variations in colour or print, either butted together or separated by lattice bands; but quilts could be made up of a collection of, say, five-patch blocks, so long as colour and print of the fabrics used tie the whole harmoniously together.

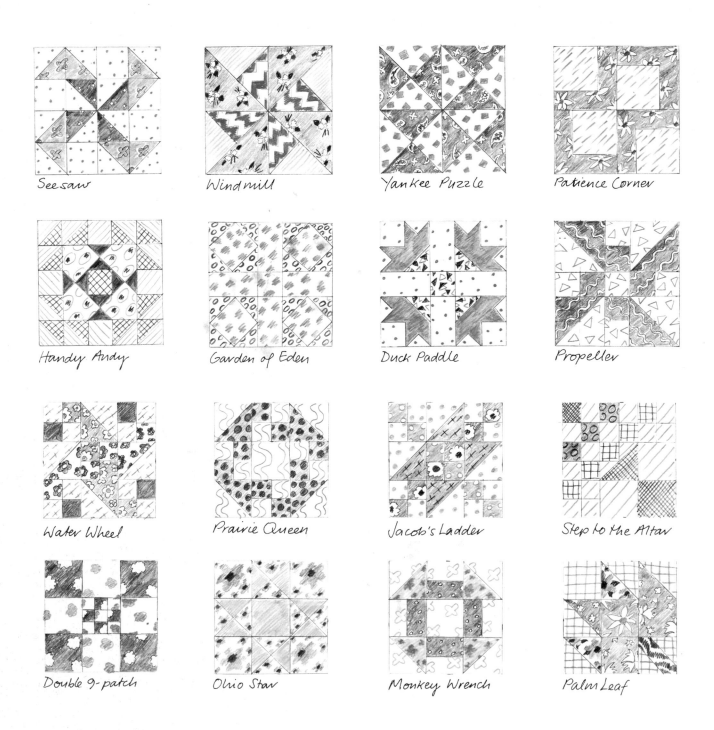

Seesaw   Windmill   Yankee Puzzle   Patience Corner

Handy Andy   Garden of Eden   Duck Paddle   Propeller

Water Wheel   Prairie Queen   Jacob's Ladder   Step to the Altar

Double 9-patch   Ohio Star   Monkey Wrench   Palm Leaf

APPLIED BLOCKS

Applied blocks range from the very simple individual flowers and leaves on some of the Baltimore Bride Quilt blocks to the very elaborate Hawaiian patterns. When complicated patterns and sharp corners make the hemming of the patch difficult, or where a fine outline is desirable as part of the design, the edges may be held down with very fine buttonhole stitch. Although this will take longer than hemming, it is a much stronger and very decorative finish.

Oak leaf

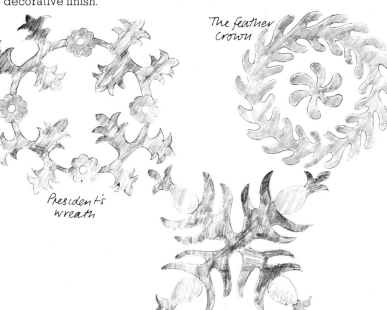
The feather crown

President's wreath

Pineapple

Cherry wreath

Princess feather

LOG CABIN DESIGNS

The simple Log Cabin blocks can be arranged in many ways, producing very different effects. For instance, the 'Straight Furrow' pattern produces diagonal bands of light and dark running across the quilt, while 'Barn Raising' (below) has concentric diamonds of light and dark surrounding a cross made by placing the dark corners of four blocks together.

PROJECTS

The following pages cover a variety of beautifully designed patchwork projects based on traditional patterns.

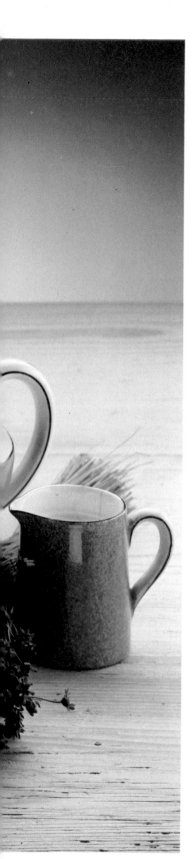

HEXAGON TEA COSY
SHOWER CAP

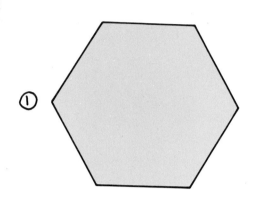

①

②

Hexagon Tea Cosy [Cozy]

30 × 23cm (12 × 9in)

MATERIALS

15 × 45cm (6 × 18in) dark cotton fabric

23 × 90cm (9 × 36in) medium-toned cotton fabric

23 × 90cm (9 × 36in) light-toned cotton fabric

45 × 90cm (18 × 36in) cotton fabric for lining

45 × 90cm (18 × 36in) synthetic wadding [batting]

76cm (30in) piping cord

Making the template

Trace the hexagon template shape in **fig. 1**. Cut it out and paste onto thin card [cardboard]. Cut out using a steel ruler and sharp knife. Alternatively, buy a ready-made template to the same dimensions. Using the template, prepare 62 pattern papers (see page 16).

Preparing the fabric

Pin pattern papers to wrong side of fabric and cut out leaving 6mm (¼in) seam allowances all round. Cut out twelve hexagons from dark fabric, twenty-four from medium-toned fabric and twenty-six from light-toned fabric. Turn seam allowances over onto pattern papers and baste in position.

Piecing the fabric

Join patches following layout in **fig. 2** to make one side of tea cosy. Make other side in the same way. Remove all pattern papers and press patchwork.

Finishing

Trim both pieces of patchwork along cutting line shown in **fig. 2**. Cut out two pieces of wadding [batting] and two pieces of lining fabric to same size. From remaining lining fabric cut a strip, 4cm (1½in) wide and 70cm (28in) long, across the grain of fabric. Fold strip in half lengthwise, wrong sides together. Place piping cord inside strip. Pin piping around edge of one of the patchwork pieces, right sides together and matching raw edges (**fig. 3**). Baste 13mm (½in) from outer edge. Pin and baste wadding [batting] to wrong side of both patchwork pieces. With right sides together, stitch both halves of tea cosy together around curved edges following basting line of piping. Turn tea cosy right side out. Turn under hem around base of tea cosy and baste in place. Taking in 13mm (½in) seam allowance, stitch lining pieces right sides together around curved edges. Turn under hem along straight edges and press (**fig. 4**). Place lining inside tea cosy and slip-stitch to patchwork all around bottom edge.

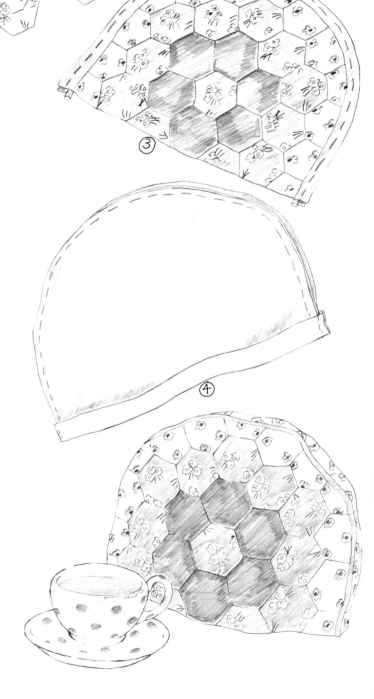

③

④

Shower Cap

To fit all sizes

MATERIALS

Approx 1m × 90cm (1yd × 36in) assorted printed cotton fabric scraps

50cm (20in) square plastic for lining

75cm (29in) narrow elastic

2m (2yd) nylon lace

Preparing the fabric

Cut twenty-five 12cm (4½in) squares out of fabric scraps.

Piecing the fabric

Taking in 6mm (¼in) seam allowances, join squares to make five rows of five squares each (**fig. 1**). Press seams open. Join the five rows together to make one large square. Press seams open.

Finishing

Make a paper pattern by cutting out a circle 49cm (19in) in diameter. Place pattern on patchwork, matching centres of circle and square (**fig. 2**). Pin and cut out. Turn under 3mm (⅛in) hem around patchwork circle and stitch. Place patchwork right side up on plastic lining and pin all around close to edge of circle. Baste lace around edge of patchwork (**fig. 3**). Stitch all three layers together as close as possible to edge of circle. Trim off excess plastic. Measure off a length of elastic to fit your head comfortably. Set sewing machine to longest stitch. Attach one end of elastic 2.5cm (1in) from edge of cap on the inside. Stitch elastic to cap, keeping 2.5cm (1in) from edge all around and pulling elastic as you go to gather fabric (**fig. 4**). Fasten off thread firmly.

cut 25 squares from scraps of patterned fabric

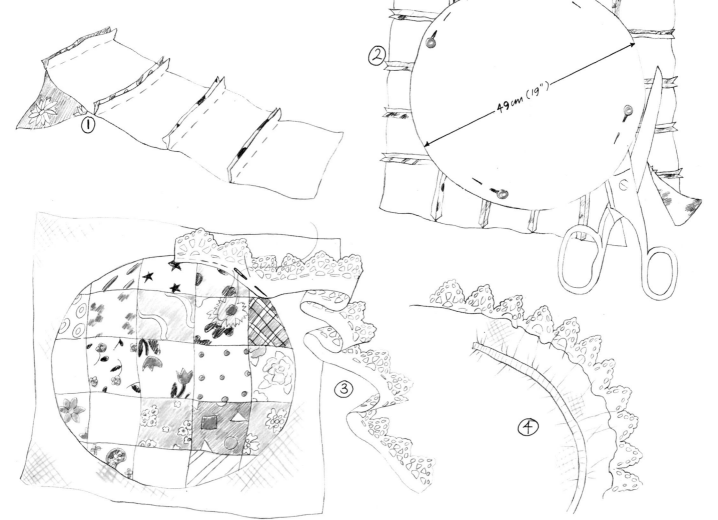

49cm (19")

NECK PURSE
COSMETIC BAG
HOLDALL

Neck Purse

16.5 × 13.5cm (6½ × 5¼in)

MATERIALS

5.5 × 43cm (2¼ × 17in) printed cotton fabric in each of 3 colours

15 × 43cm (6 × 17in) plain cotton fabric for lining

2m (2yd) bias binding

15 × 43cm (6 × 17in) synthetic wadding [batting]

1 toggle button

Piecing the fabric

Join the three strips of printed cotton fabric together lengthwise, taking in 6mm (¼in) seam allowances (**fig. 1**). Press seams open.

Quilting

Place wadding [batting] on wrong side of lining fabric. Place patchwork right side up on top of wadding [batting]. Pin all three layers together. Baste firmly around edges. Machine or hand quilt along seamlines and around raw edges (**fig. 2**). Trim off excess wadding [batting] and lining fabric.

Finishing

Sew bias binding along one of the short sides of fabric (**fig. 3**). Cut 12cm (4½in) bias binding for toggle loop. Fold lengthwise and stich edges together. Fold purse allowing 9cm (3½in) for flap (**fig. 4**). Baste side seams together. Fold toggle loop in half and baste to inside flap centre (**fig. 4**). Stitch side seams and around flap, gently curving corners and attaching toggle loop. Trim off excess fabric close to stitching line. Sew bias binding around edges of purse. Cut a 76cm (30in) length of bias binding for neck strap. Fold lengthwise and stitch edges together. Attach ends of strap to outside of purse behind fold line on either side. Fold over flap and sew toggle button in position on purse front (**fig. 5**).

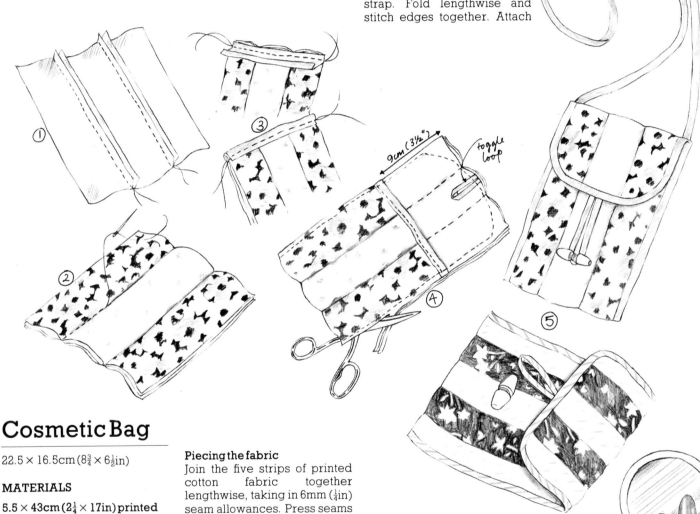

Cosmetic Bag

22.5 × 16.5cm (8¾ × 6½in)

MATERIALS

5.5 × 43cm (2¼ × 17in) printed cotton fabric in each of the 5 colours

23.5 × 43cm (9¼ × 17in) plastic for lining

1.5m (1½yd) bias binding

23.5 × 43cm (9¼ × 17in) synthetic wadding [batting]

1 toggle button

Piecing the fabric

Join the five strips of printed cotton fabric together lengthwise, taking in 6mm (¼in) seam allowances. Press seams open.

Quilting

Place patchwork right side up on top of wadding [batting]. Pin and baste firmly around edges. Machine or hand quilt along seamlines and around raw edges. Trim off excess wadding [batting].

Finishing

Place fabric right side up on wrong side of plastic lining. Baste all round, keeping close to edges of fabric to avoid tearing plastic. Machine stitch along basting line. Trim off excess plastic. Finish as for neck purse, omitting strap.

Holdall
[Carryall]

$46 \times 25.5 \times 15.5$cm ($18 \times 10 \times$ 6in)

MATERIALS

11 strips assorted cotton fabric 5.5×89cm ($2\frac{1}{4} \times 35$in)

10 strips assorted cotton fabric 5.5×30cm ($2\frac{1}{4} \times 12$in)

46×67cm (18×27in) printed cotton fabric for straps

100×90cm (36×36in) plain cotton fabric for lining

2m (2yd) seam binding

100×90cm (36×36in) synthetic wadding [batting]

46cm (18in) zipper

Piecing the fabric

For body of bag join the eleven longer strips together lengthwise, taking in 6mm ($\frac{1}{4}$in) seam allowances (**fig. 1**). Press seams open. For gussets join five of the shorter strips together lengthwise, taking in 6mm ($\frac{1}{4}$in) seam allowances. Press seams open. Repeat with remaining five strips.

Quilting

Place wadding [batting] on wrong side of lining fabric. Lay out patchwork pieces on top of wadding [batting], right sides up. Pin and cut lining fabric and wadding [batting] to size of patchwork pieces. Baste around raw edges of each piece through all three layers. Machine or hand quilt along seamlines and around raw edges of each piece.

Finishing

Make a paper pattern for the bag gussets by cutting out a rectangle 28×18cm (11×7in), trimming each corner into a gentle curve. Place pattern on one of quilted gusset pieces and draw around edge with a soft pencil. Machine stitch along drawn line (**fig. 2**). Trim excess fabric back to stitching line. Repeat with remaining gusset piece. Cut fabric for straps into 12cm ($4\frac{1}{2}$in) wide strips. Join strips together to

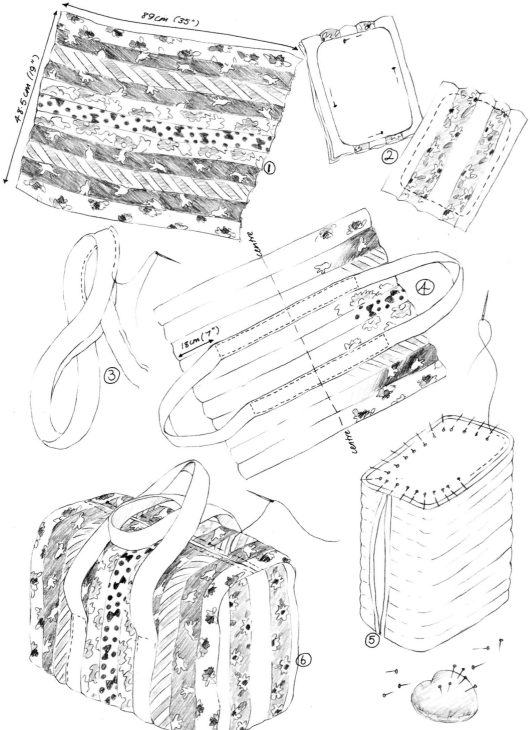

make one continuous strip 254cm (100in) long. Turn under 6mm ($\frac{1}{4}$in) hems along both edges and press. Fold strip in half lengthwise, wrong sides together. Press. Cut remaining wadding [batting] into 4.5cm ($1\frac{3}{4}$in) wide strips and join to make one long strip to fit strap. Place wadding [batting] inside

strap. Pin and baste edges (**fig. 3**). Stitch strap 3mm ($\frac{1}{8}$in) from both edges. Mark centre lines of strap and bag body (**fig. 4**). Place strap on fourth strip from the edge of bag on each side, matching centre markings. Stitch strap to bag body along the lines of strips to within 18cm (7in) of edges of bag (**fig. 4**).

Turn under a double hem 2cm ($\frac{3}{4}$in) deep along short sides of bag body. With right sides together, pin and baste gusset pieces to long sides of bag body (**fig. 5**). Stitch seams. Remove basting stitches and bind seam edges. Turn bag right side out and finally insert zipper in opening (**fig. 6**).

CATHEDRAL WINDOW PURSE

OCCASIONAL BAG

There are two methods for making up Cathedral Window patchwork – the traditional method and a slightly quicker modern method using machine stitching or running stitch. Both methods are described on page 24. It is a matter of personal preference which one you choose.

The 'occasional' bag is another easy pattern for beginners. It is made up from simple triangular patterns joined together into strips. The finished bag is a useful shape for keeping sewing accessories and knitting wools.

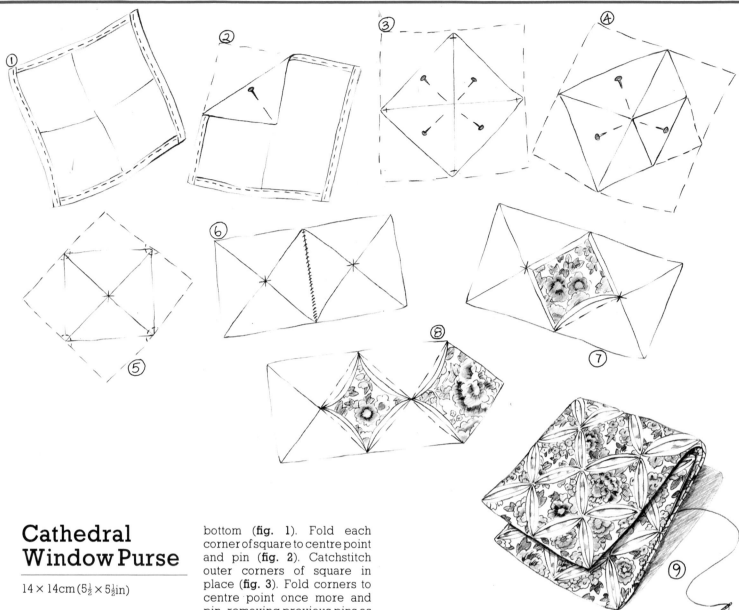

Cathedral Window Purse

14 × 14cm (5½ × 5½in)

MATERIALS

30 × 90cm (12 × 36in) cream cotton fabric

18 × 36cm (7 × 14in) printed cotton fabric

17 × 43cm (6½ × 17in) cotton fabric for lining

Preparing the fabric

Cut out twelve 15cm (6in) squares from the cream fabric. Cut out thirty-two 4.5cm (1¾in) squares from the printed fabric.

Piecing the fabric

Take a cream fabric square and turn under and baste a 6mm (¼in) hem on all four sides. With wrong side facing, find centre of square by folding it in half left to right then top to bottom (**fig. 1**). Fold each corner of square to centre point and pin (**fig. 2**). Catchstitch outer corners of square in place (**fig. 3**). Fold corners to centre point once more and pin, removing previous pins as you go (**fig. 4**). Catchstitch outer corners of square in place. Stabstitch opposite points together at centre (**fig. 5**). An alternative method of reaching this stage [step] is shown on page 24. Prepare remaining eleven cream patches in the same way. Take two prepared squares and oversew [overcast] together down one side (**fig. 6**). Repeat with remaining five pairs of squares. Join the six pairs of squares together to make a rectangle six squares by two. Place a square of printed fabric over vertical join [joining] in each pair of squares. Fold back cream fabric onto printed square along all four sides and slipstitch in place (**fig. 7**). Place remaining printed squares along edge of fabric as shown in **fig. 8**. Fold over cream fabric along two sides of each square and slipstitch in place. Fold other half of printed square to back of patchwork and catchstitch in place. Remove any visible basting stitches.

Finishing

Measure patchwork and cut lining fabric to fit, adding 13mm (½in) seam allowances all round. Turn under seam allowances and press. With wrong sides together, slipstitch lining to patchwork down both long sides and oversew [overcast] along short sides. Fold bag in three. Oversew [overcast] side seams (**fig. 9**).

CATHEDRAL WINDOW VARIATIONS

Cushion [pillow] covers

A cover for a 40 × 40cm (16 × 16in) cushion can be made from thirty-six squares made to same dimensions as the purse squares and using a plain fabric for backing.

Bedcovers

It is not essential to line cathedral window patchwork used for bedcovers if, instead of turning the edging print squares to the back of the work, they are folded back on themselves and the edges slipstitched in place. This makes the backing much neater.

Occasional Bag

40 × 25cm (16 × 10in)

MATERIALS

10 × 90cm (4 × 36in) printed cotton fabric in each of 4 different colours

40 × 56cm (16 × 22in) cotton lining fabric

Two 30cm (12in) long wooden handles

Making the template

Trace template shape in **fig. 1**. Cut out and paste onto thin card [cardboard]. Cut out using a steel ruler and sharp knife.

Preparing the fabric

Using template, mark and cut out seventy triangles from the various prints, adding 6mm ($\frac{1}{4}$in) seam allowances around each one. Use cutting layout shown in **fig. 2** for maximum economy of fabric.

Piecing the fabric

Join pairs of triangles together to make squares, taking in 6mm ($\frac{1}{4}$in) seam allowances (**fig. 3**). Press all seams to one side. Join squares together in rows of five, keeping diagonal seams in same direction and seam allowances pressed to same side (**fig. 4**). Press vertical seams open. Join rows together, pinning seams to ensure accurate fit (**fig. 5**). Press horizontal seams open.

Finishing

Measure patchwork and cut lining fabric to fit. Place patchwork and lining right sides together and stitch along three sides. Turn right side out. Slip-stitch along fourth side. Place one end of bag through slot in wooden handle (**fig. 6**). Turn over edge to inside and stitch down, bunching up [gathering] fabric to allow for fullness (**fig. 7**). Attach second handle to opposite side of bag in the same way (**fig. 8**). Fold bag in half, right sides together. Stitch from fold to within 10cm (4in) of handles on each side of bag. Turn bag right side out (**fig. 9**).
Note:
Sandwich wadding [batting] between layers to quilt bag.

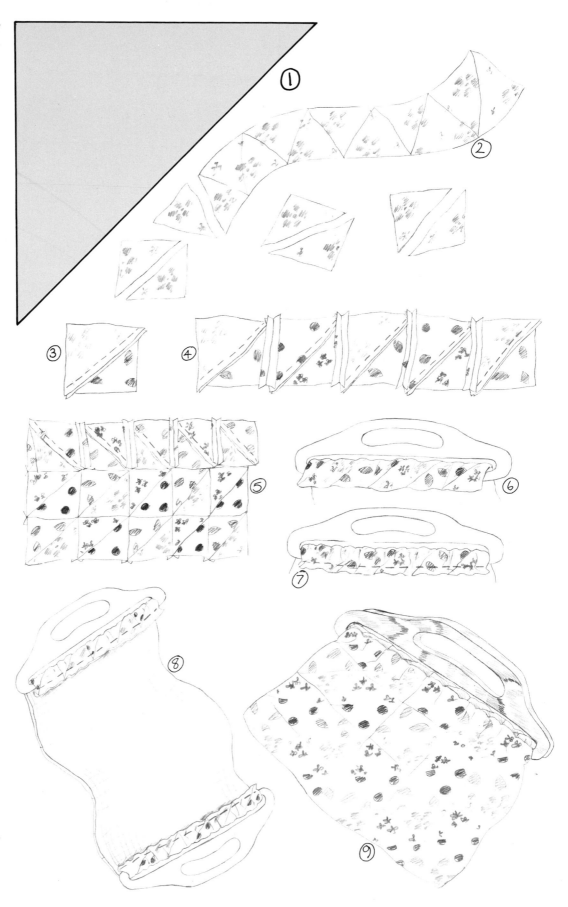

SEWING CASE
PINCUSHION
CLAMSHELL
CUSHION COVER

The colours for these three projects must be chosen with care.

To make up the pincushion to look like the ones in the photograph, you will need to select patterns using a window template. The method for this is described on page 18.

The success of the clamshell cushion [pillow] cover also relies on the careful arrangement of the coloured patches. Instructions for piecing clamshell patches are given in detail on page 22.

Sewing Case

15 × 40cm (6 × 16in)

MATERIALS

18 × 90cm (7 × 36in) dark coloured cotton or silk fabric

14 × 90cm (5½ × 36in) medium coloured cotton or silk fabric

55 × 90cm (22 × 36in) light coloured cotton or silk fabric

40 × 90cm (16 × 36in) lightweight calico [muslin] for interlining

16 × 42cm (6½ × 17in) thin foam rubber sheeting

80cm (32in) narrow ribbon

4 press [snap] fasteners

Making the templates

Trace shapes in **fig. 1**. Cut out and paste onto thin card [cardboard]. Cut out using a steel ruler and sharp knife. Use templates to cut out the appropriate numbers of pattern papers.

Preparing the fabric

Pin pattern papers to wrong side of fabric and cut out, adding 6mm (¼in) seam allowances all around. Cut twenty-seven diamonds from dark fabric, twenty-seven diamonds from light fabric and twenty diamonds from medium fabric. Cut out the remaining shapes from medium fabric. Turn seam allowances over onto pattern papers. Baste and press.

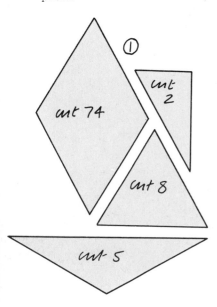

Piecing the fabric

Join patches following layout in **fig. 2**. When all the patches have been joined, remove pattern papers and basting threads.

Finishing

Make paper patterns following diagrams in **fig. 3**. Cut out one of each shape in light fabric and interlining. From interlining only, cut a rectangle 19 × 45cm (7½ × 18in). Place matching pairs of light fabric and interlining right sides together and stitch along stitching lines. Clip at each end of stitching lines as shown. Turn each pair right side out and press. Fold under 15mm (⅝in) on raw edges opposite curved edges and slipstitch together (**fig. 4**). Finish one of long sides of 11cm (4½in) piece in the same way. Attach press [snap] fastener tops and bottoms as shown in **fig. 3**. Do up press [snap] fasteners when attached. Place pocket fronts on interlining rectangle and stitch down flaps. Fold ribbon in half and attach to one end of pocket strip. Baste foam sheeting to wrong side of patchwork. Stitch patchwork to pocket strip, right sides together, taking in 15mm (⅝in) seam allowance along three sides, leaving ribbon end open. Turn right side out. Slipstitch open side. Roll up bag and tie ribbon.

②

③ 7½cm (3") — 19cm (7½") — 18cm (7¼")

19cm (7½") 6cm (2⅜") centre line 6cm (2⅜")

clip 1½cm (⅝") clip clip

19cm (7½") 6cm (2⅜") centre line ④ 1½cm (⅝")

17cm (6¾") 11½cm (4½")

clip

O Press stud top
● Press stud bottom

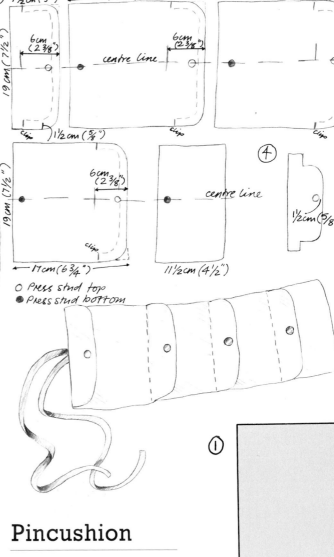

Pincushion

10 × 11.5cm (4 × 4½in)

MATERIALS

Assorted scraps printed cotton fabric

Stiff cardboard

Synthetic wadding [batting]

Making the templates

Trace the shapes in **fig. 1**. Cut out and paste onto thin card [cardboard]. Cut out using a steel ruler and sharp knife. Prepare six pattern papers from each shape (see page 16).

Preparing the fabric

Lay pattern papers on wrong side of appropriate fabric scraps. Pin and cut out allowing 6mm (¼in) seam allowances all round. Turn over seam allowances onto pattern papers and baste firmly.

① cut 74

cut 2

cut 8

cut 5

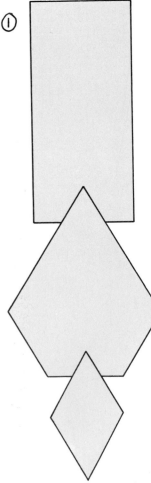

Clamshell Cushion [Pillow] Cover

35 × 35cm (12 × 12in)

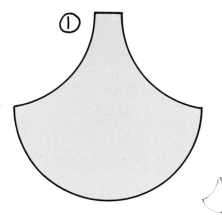

MATERIALS

50 × 90cm (20 × 36in) plain cotton fabric in each of 4 tones of 1 colour

50 × 90cm (20 × 36in) plain cotton in darker tone for backing

23cm (10in) zipper

Making the template

Trace the shape in **fig. 1**. Cut out and paste onto thin card. Cut out using a steel ruler and sharp knife. Alternatively buy a ready-made template. Prepare 100 pattern papers – exactly the same size.

Preparing the fabric

To prepare each clamshell patch, lay fabric face down on flat surface. Pin pattern papers to fabric. Cut out, adding 6mm (¼in) seam allowance all round. Turn over seam allowance onto pattern papers and baste securely through all layers. Prepare 20 patches in the dark fabric, 32 in the medium dark fabric, 28 in the medium light fabric, and 20 in the light fabric.

Piecing the fabric

Join the patches following the layout in **fig. 2** (see page 22). Remove all pattern papers and press patchwork.

Finishing

Trim the patchwork around edges to neaten. Cut out two pieces of backing fabric, measuring half the size of patchwork top plus 13mm (½in) seam allowance along one side. Join seam leaving 23cm (10in) open in centre. Press seam open. Insert zipper in opening. Place patchwork on backing, right sides together, with zipper closed. Seam together around all four edges. Open zipper and turn right side out.

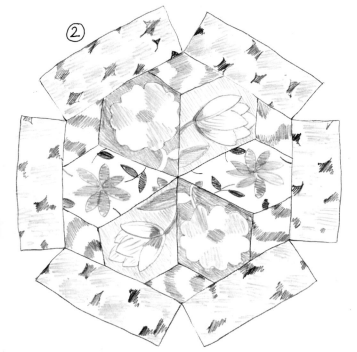

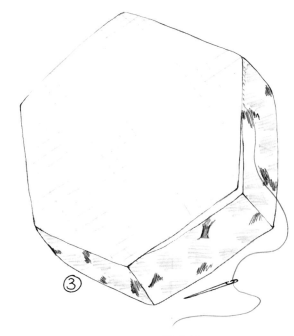

Piecing the fabric

Join patches as shown in **fig. 2** (see page 17). First join the six pentagons, then the diamond shapes and finally the rectangles.. Press well on both sides. Remove pattern papers from pentagons and diamonds. Join side seams of rectangles.

Finishing

Construct a 5.5cm (2¼in) sided hexagon on the stiff cardboard (see page 12) and cut it out. Cover with fabric, stitching from corner to corner on the wrong side with strong thread. Oversew [overcast] hexagon base neatly to pieced top of pincushion leaving two sides open for stuffing (**fig. 3**). Stuff with wadding [batting] and sew up opening.

STAR & SQUARE CUSHION COVERS

Star Cushion [Pillow] Cover

46 × 46cm (18 × 18in)

MATERIALS

20 × 30cm (8 × 12in) printed cotton fabric for star

10 × 90cm (4 × 36in) printed cotton fabric in each of 5 colours

50cm (20in) square of synthetic wadding [batting]

50cm (20in) square cotton fabric for interlining

50 × 60cm (20 × 24in) cotton fabric for backing

20 × 90cm (8 × 36in) printed cotton fabric for binding

40cm (16in) zipper

Making the templates

Trace the shapes in **fig. 1**. Add 1cm (⅜in) seam allowances, then cut out and paste onto thin card [cardboard]. Cut out using a steel ruler and sharp knife.

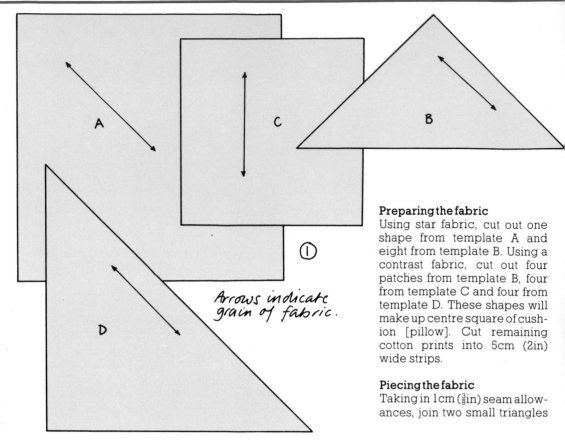

Arrows indicate grain of fabric.

Preparing the fabric

Using star fabric, cut out one shape from template A and eight from template B. Using a contrast fabric, cut out four patches from template B, four from template C and four from template D. These shapes will make up centre square of cushion [pillow]. Cut remaining cotton prints into 5cm (2in) wide strips.

Piecing the fabric

Taking in 1cm (⅜in) seam allowances, join two small triangles

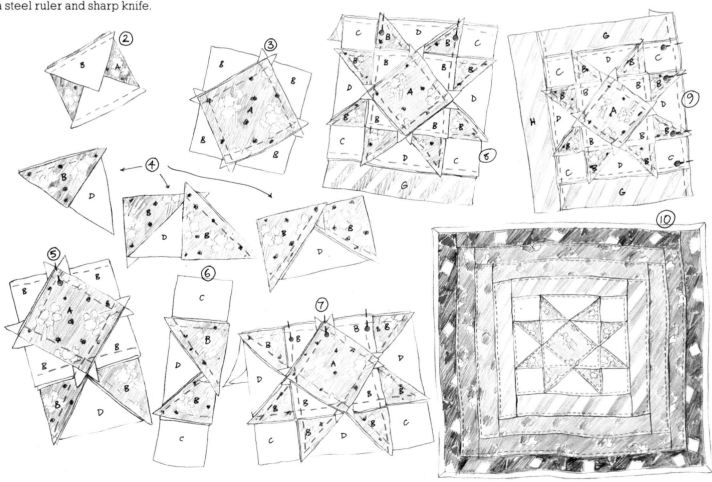

(B) in contrast fabric to opposite sides of A (**fig. 2**). Join two similar triangles to other two sides of A (**fig. 3**). Press all seams outwards as you work. Join small triangles to large triangles to make four oblong patches (**fig. 4**). Join two oblong patches to opposite sides of square patch (**fig. 5**). Join small squares (C) to either end of two remaining oblong patches (**fig. 6**). Join these three strips to make up star (**fig. 7**). Join a 5cm (2in) wide strip to top and bottom of square, trimming off surplus strip (**fig. 8**). Join a 5cm (2in) wide strip in same fabric to both sides of patchwork (**fig. 9**). Join three more borders in the same way. Press all seams outwards as you work.

Quilting

Measure patchwork and cut wadding [batting] and interlining slightly larger all around. Sandwich wadding [batting] between patchwork and interlining, wrong sides together. Pin and baste all three layers together, working from centre outwards. Baste firmly around edges. Quilt along lines shown in **fig. 10**, working from centre outwards.

Finishing

Cut out two pieces of backing fabric, measuring half the size of patchwork top plus 13mm (½in) seam allowance along one side. Join seam, leaving 40cm (16in) open in centre (**fig. 11**). Press seam open. Insert zipper in opening (**fig. 12**). Cut binding fabric into 6cm (2¼in) wide strips. Join strips to make one strip long enough to go round edges of cushion [pillow]. Fold strip in half lengthwise, wrong sides together, and press to make double binding for extra strength. Place patchwork on backing, wrong sides together, with zipper closed. Baste together around all four edges. Pin binding around cushion [pillow] cover through all layers, right sides together and matching raw edges. Stitch binding to cushion [pillow] cover and mitre corners (see page 25). Trim off excess fabric. Turn binding to back of cushion [pillow] and hem along stitching line.

Square Cushion [Pillow] Cover

46 × 46cm (18 × 18in)

MATERIALS

30 × 30cm (12 × 12in) printed cotton fabric for centre square (A)

10 × 90cm (4 × 36in) printed cotton fabric in each of 4 colours (B,C,D,E)

20 × 90cm (8 × 36in) cotton fabric for binding

50cm (20) square cotton fabric for interlining

50 × 60cm (20 × 24in) cotton fabric for backing

50cm (20in) square of synthetic wadding [batting]

40cm (16in) zipper

Preparing the fabric

From fabric A, cut out one 22cm (8⅝in) square and four 5cm (2in) squares. From fabric B, cut out four 5cm (2in) wide strips 22cm (8⅝in) long and four 5cm (2in) squares. From fabric C, cut out four 5cm (2in) wide strips 28cm (11in) long and four 5cm (2in) squares. From fabric D, cut out four 5cm (2in) wide strips 34cm (13⅜in) long and four 5cm (2in) wide squares. From fabric E, cut out four 5cm (2in) wide strips 40cm (15¾in) long.

Piecing the fabric

Taking in 1cm (⅜in) seam allowances, join one B strip to opposite sides of large square (**fig. 1**). Press seams outwards. Join one small square in A to either end of two remaining B strips (**fig. 2**). Join these two strips to either side of large square (**fig. 3**). Press seams outwards. Join one C strip to opposite sides of patchwork square. Join one small square in B to either end of remaining C strips. Join these two strips to either side of patchwork (**fig. 4**). Press seams outwards. Join remaining strips and squares in the same way using **fig. 5** as a guide.

Quilting and finishing

Quilt and finish cushion [pillow] cover as for star cushion [pillow] but following quilting lines in **fig. 5**.

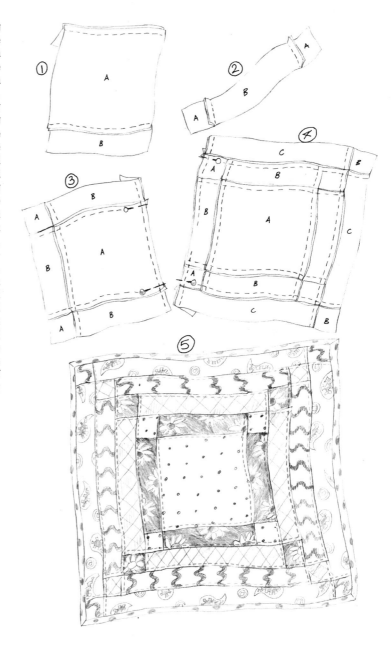

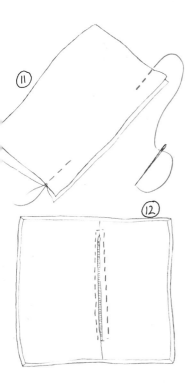

MICHELE'S QUILT
FRUIT BASKET
CUSHION COVER

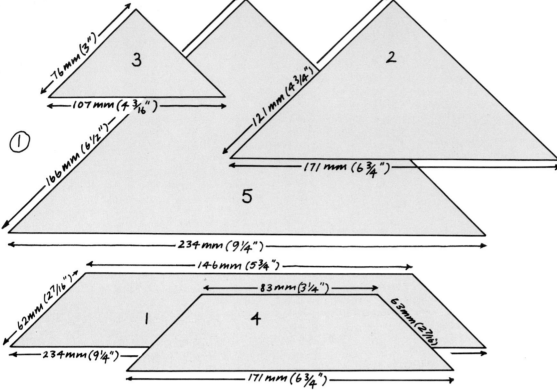

① 3 — 76mm (3") — 107mm (4 3/16") — 166mm (6 1/2")

2 — 121mm (4 3/4")

5 — 171mm (6 3/4") — 234mm (9 1/4")

1 — 146mm (5 3/4") — 62mm (2 7/16") — 234mm (9 1/4")

4 — 83mm (3 1/4") — 63mm (2 7/16") — 171mm (6 3/4")

④

Fig. 4 shows the layout of patches for border block. Join patches together, taking in 6mm ($\frac{1}{4}$in) seam allowances and following sequence shown in

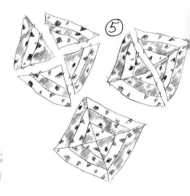

⑤

fig. 5. Press seams towards darker patches where possible. Press diagonal seams open.

Michele's Quilt

2.36 × 1.78m (93 × 70in)

MATERIALS

2m × 90cm (2yd × 36in) light cotton fabric (A)

2m × 90cm (2yd × 36in) light cotton fabric (B)

4m × 90cm (4$\frac{1}{2}$yd × 36in) dark cotton fabric (C)

4m × 90cm (4$\frac{1}{2}$yd × 36in) dark cotton fabric (D)

6m × 90cm (6$\frac{1}{2}$yd × 36in) cotton fabric for lining

Making the templates

Copy shapes in **fig. 1** full size on graph paper. Cut out and paste onto thin card [cardboard]. Cut out using a steel ruler and sharp knife. Label templates as shown. Templates 1 and 2 are used for the main block. Templates 1, 3 and 4 are used for the border blocks. Template 5 is a filler.

Preparing the fabric

For each main block you will need four shapes cut from template 1, two in fabric C and two in fabric D, and four shapes cut from template 2, two in fabric A and two in fabric B. For the border blocks you will need

four shapes from template 1, two in fabric C and two in fabric D; four shapes from template 3, two in fabric C and two in fabric D; and four shapes from template 4, two in fabric C and two in fabric D. Cut out shapes, adding 6mm ($\frac{1}{4}$in) seam allowances all round each one. Prepare enough patches for fifty-nine main blocks and twenty-four border blocks (see plan, **fig. 7**). Using template 5, cut out twenty-six shapes in fabric C and twenty-six in fabric D.

Piecing the fabric

Fig. 2 shows the layout of patches for main block. Join

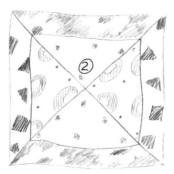

②

patches together, taking in 6mm ($\frac{1}{4}$in) seam allowances and following sequence shown in **fig. 3**. Press seams towards dark patches where possible. Press diagonal seams open.

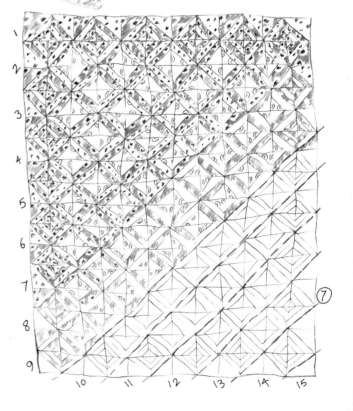

⑦

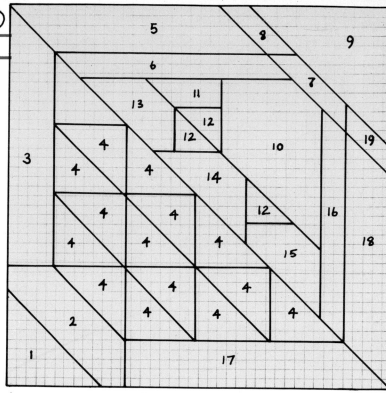

Join filler patches in pairs (**fig. 6**), leaving four single patches for corners. Assemble blocks following layout in **fig. 7**. First join them to make fifteen rows. Press seams towards darker fabric. Join rows. Press seams open.

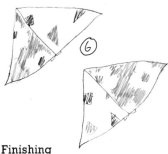

Finishing

Measure patchwork. Seam lining fabric together to fit, adding 4cm (1½in) all round for border. Lay lining face down on flat surface. Place patchwork right side up on top, matching centres. Baste the two layers together around edges. Fold overlapping lining fabric to front of patchwork. Turn under 13mm (½in) hem all round, leaving border of about 25mm (1in) on all sides. Mitre corners. Baste borders to patchwork and secure with running stitch through both layers or decorative embroidery.

Fruit Basket Cushion [Pillow] Cover

50 × 50cm (20 × 20in)

MATERIALS

60 × 90cm (24 × 36in) plain cotton fabric in main colour

30 × 90cm (12 × 36in) plain cotton fabric in each of 4 contrast colours

Assorted cotton scraps in fruit colours

60cm (24in) square cotton calico backing fabric

60cm (24in) square synthetic wadding [batting]

40cm (16in) zipper

Making the templates

Copy the design in **fig. 1** full size on graph paper. Cut out one of each numbered shape and paste onto thin card [cardboard]. Cut out shapes using a steel ruler and sharp knife. Number templates as shown.

Preparing the fabric

For each fruit basket block, cut nine shapes from template 4 and one each from templates 2, 6, 7 and 16, all from the same colour fabric to form the framework and handle of basket. Cut six shapes from template 4 in a contrast colour for the rest of basket. Cut one shape from each of templates 1, 3, 5, 8, 9, 10, 11, 17, 18, 19 and two shapes from template 12 from same colour fabric to form background. Cut one shape from templates 13, 14 and 15 in fruit colours and one from template 12 for the leaf. Vary colours from block to block as required. Cut out each shape, adding 6mm (¼in) seam allowances all around. Prepare enough patches for four blocks. Following patterns in **fig. 2**, cut out four outer border strips in main colour and four inner border strips in contrast colour.

Piecing the fabric

For each block, join pairs of triangles in contrast colours to make five squares (**fig. 3**). Press seams open. Construct lower half of block by making progressively larger units as

shown in **fig. 4**. Construct upper half of block in a similar manner following **fig. 5**. Join two halves of block. Piece the remaining three blocks in the same way. Press all seams open at each stage [step]. Join blocks together to make large square. Join inner border strips to outer border strips along 45cm (18in) edges. Join all four corners of borders, leaving inner 6mm (¼in) seam allowances unstitched (**fig. 6**). Set pieced blocks into border, taking in seam allowances all around.

Quilting

Cut wadding [batting] and calico backing fabric slightly larger than patchwork all round. Sandwich wadding [batting] between calico and patchwork. Pin and baste the three layers together working from centre outwards. Stitch through all layers following joins [joinings] between patches and sinking [hiding] stitches in seam lines. Trim off excess wadding [batting] and backing fabric.

Finishing

Cut back of cushion [pillow] to fit from remaining fabric in main colour. With right sides facing, seam backing to patchwork along three sides. Turn right side out. Insert zipper.

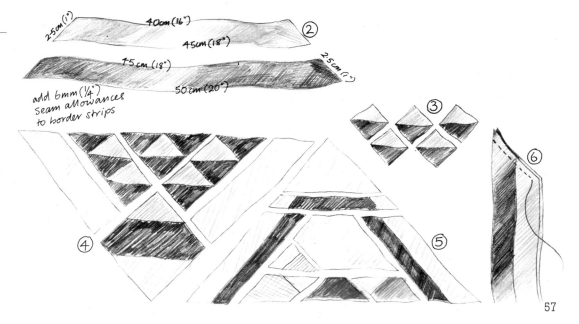

1 square = 5mm (5 squares = 1")

add 6mm (¼") seam allowances to border strips

ALPHABET COT QUILT

The letters and numerals on this charming quilt are applied by hand. Each character is outlined with stitching to give a padded appearance. The squares are joined by narrow bands and the quilt is finished with a matching binding.

To make the quilt you will need to enlarge the letters and numerals to the correct size. The shapes are printed on a grid, each square of which is equivalent to 13mm (½inch). In order to enlarge the design to scale you will need graph paper ruled in 13mm (½inch) squares. To copy a character, position each line within the 13mm (½inch) square corresponding to the small square in which it falls on the printed page.

ABCDEF
GHIJKL
MNOPQ
RSTUVW
XYZ123
456789

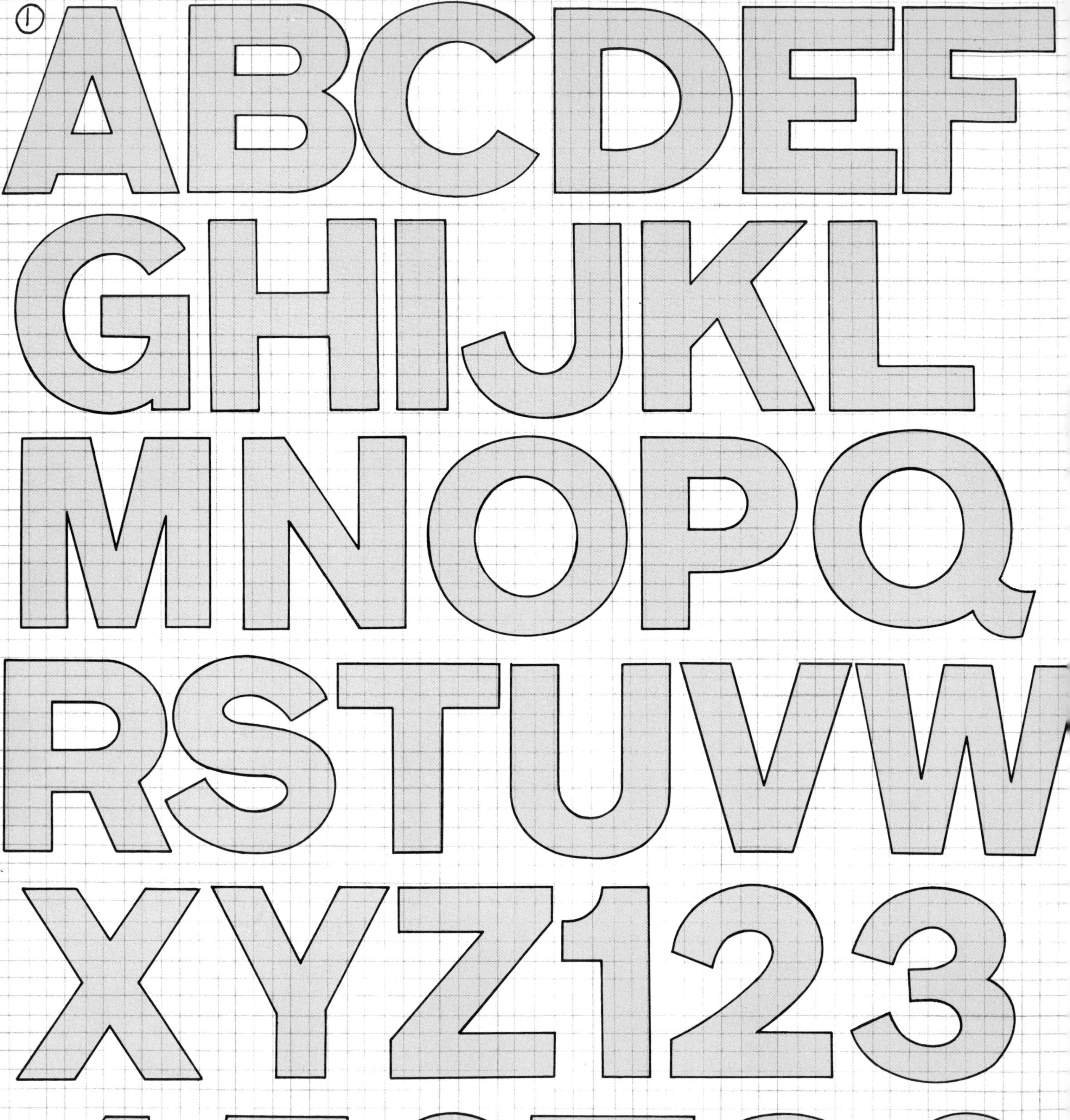

1 square = 13mm (½")

quilting lines

④

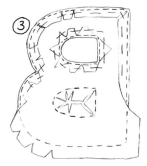

82cm (32½in) long, and twenty-eight 3cm (1¼in) wide bands 17cm (6¾in) long.

Appliquéing the characters

Turn under 6mm (¼in) around each character (**fig. 3**). Baste and press. Place one character on each of the plain cotton squares and hem in position.

③

Piecing the fabric

Following layout in **fig. 4** and taking in 1cm (⅜in) seam allowances, join appliquéd squares in rows of five separated by four short bands. Press seams towards bands. Join rows to make seven rows separated by six long bands. Press seams towards bands.

Quilting

Measure patchwork and cut wadding [batting] and lining fabric slightly larger all around. Sandwich wadding [batting] between lining and patchwork, wrong sides together. Pin and baste all three layers together, working from centre outwards. Baste firmly around edges. Starting in centre with 'R', quilt by hand or machine along lines shown in fig. 4. Outline squares first, then the characters.

Finishing

Cut binding fabric into 6cm (2½ in) wide strips. Join strips to make one strip long enough to go round edges of quilt. Fold strip lengthwise, wrong sides together, and press to make double binding for extra strength. Pin binding around quilt, right sides together, and matching raw edges. Stitch binding to quilt and mitre corners (see page 25). Trim off excess wadding [batting] and lining fabric. Turn over binding to wrong side of quilt and hem along stitching line.

Alphabet Cot Quilt

1.13m × 81cm (45 × 32in)

MATERIALS

1.4m × 90cm (55 × 36in) plain cotton fabric

Approx 1.4m × 90cm (55 × 36in) assorted scraps in printed cotton fabric

1.3m × 90cm (51 × 36in) cotton fabric for lining

70 × 90cm (28 × 36in) cotton fabric for bands and binding

1.3m × 90cm (51 × 36in) synthetic wadding [batting]

Making the templates

Copy letters and numerals in **fig. 1** full size on graph paper. Cut out and paste onto thin card [cardboard]. Cut out using a steel ruler and sharp knife.

Preparing the fabric

From plain fabric, cut out thirty-five 17cm (6¾in) squares. Lay templates for numbers and letters, wrong side up, on wrong side of printed cotton scraps. Trace around each one with a soft pencil. *Do not cut them out.* Machine stitch carefully on drawn lines to outline each character. Cut out characters adding 6mm (¼in) seam allowances all around. Clip into all curves and corners (**fig. 2**). From band fabric, cut out six 3cm (1¼in) wide bands

②

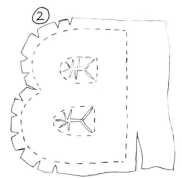

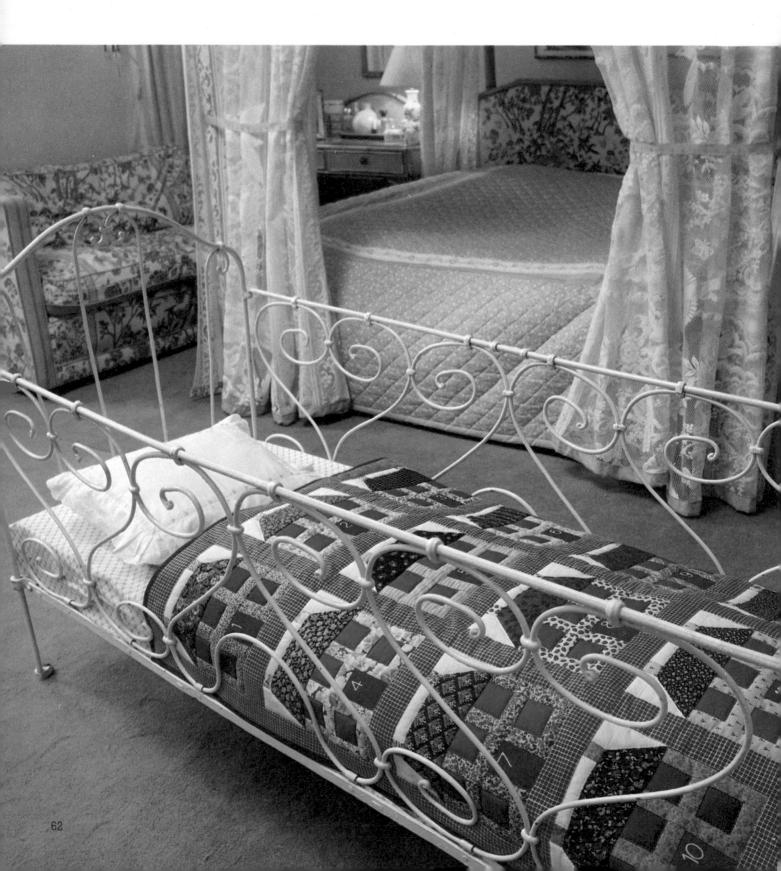

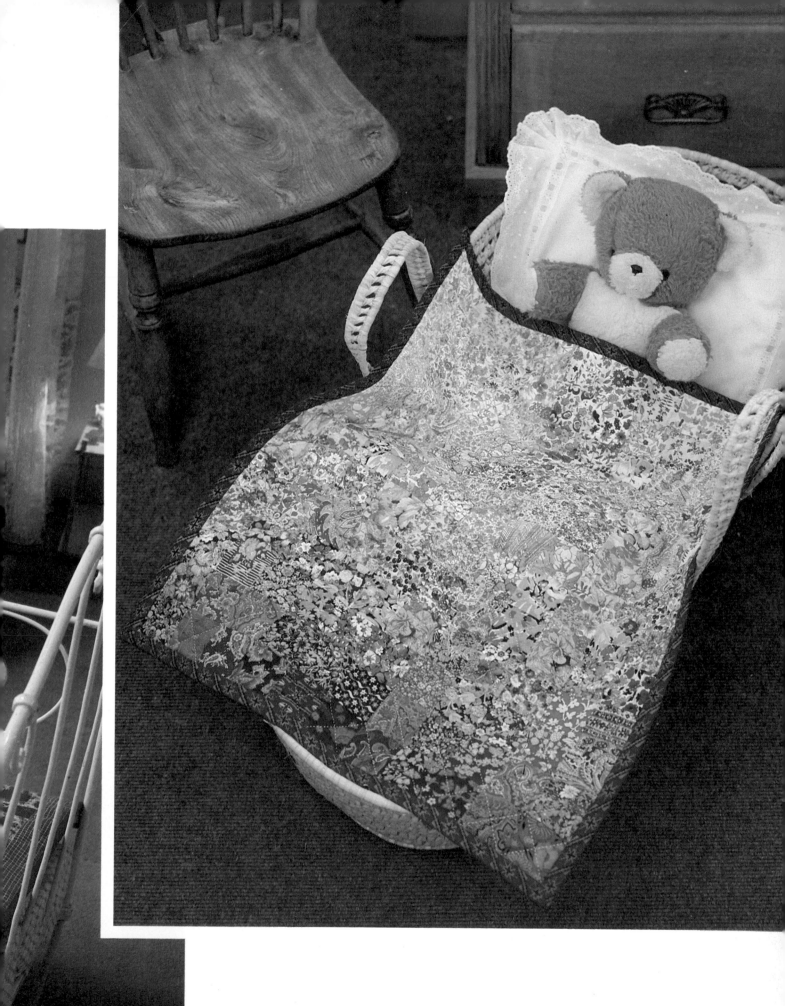

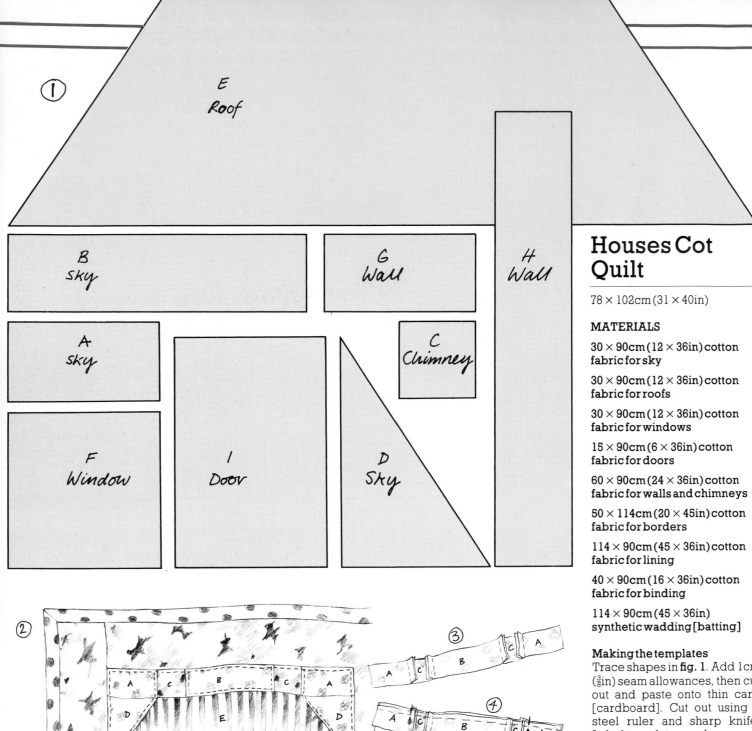

Houses Cot Quilt

78 × 102cm (31 × 40in)

MATERIALS

30 × 90cm (12 × 36in) cotton fabric for sky

30 × 90cm (12 × 36in) cotton fabric for roofs

30 × 90cm (12 × 36in) cotton fabric for windows

15 × 90cm (6 × 36in) cotton fabric for doors

60 × 90cm (24 × 36in) cotton fabric for walls and chimneys

50 × 114cm (20 × 45in) cotton fabric for borders

114 × 90cm (45 × 36in) cotton fabric for lining

40 × 90cm (16 × 36in) cotton fabric for binding

114 × 90cm (45 × 36in) synthetic wadding [batting]

Making the templates

Trace shapes in **fig. 1**. Add 1cm ($\frac{3}{8}$in) seam allowances, then cut out and paste onto thin card [cardboard]. Cut out using a steel ruler and sharp knife. Label templates as shown.

Preparing the fabric

For each house block, using appropriate fabrics, cut out two shapes from template A, one from template B, two from template C, one from template D and another from template D reversed, one from template E, five from templates F and G, four from template H and one from template I. Cut border fabric into 6cm ($2\frac{3}{8}$in) wide strips. Make up two strips 105cm (41in) long, five strips 70cm (28in) long and eight strips 22cm ($8\frac{3}{4}$in) long.

64

Piecing the fabric

Make up a house block following layout in **fig. 2** and taking in 1cm (⅜in) seam allowances all round. First join A, B and C patches (**fig. 3**). Press seams towards C's. Join one D either side of E. Join these two strips together (**fig. 4**). Press seam towards roof. Make each side of house separately, joining F and G patches in vertical strips. Press seams towards walls. Join H patches to either side of each strip (**fig. 5**). Press seams towards H. Join F, G and I patches. Press seams towards G. Join sides of house either side of door strip. Press seams towards H. Join roof to house. Press seams towards roof. Make up eleven more house blocks in the same way. Embroider door numbers on each house if desired. Join house blocks together in rows of three, each house separated by a 22cm (8¾in) border strip. Join rows together each one separated from the next by a 70cm (28in) border strip. Join another 70cm (28in) strip at top and bottom of patchwork. Join 105cm (41in) border strip down each side. Press all seams towards border strips.

Quilting

Measure patchwork and cut wadding [batting] and lining fabric slightly larger all around. Sandwich wadding [batting] between lining and patchwork, wrong sides together. Pin and baste all three layers together, working from centre outwards. Baste firmly around all four sides. Quilt along lines shown in **fig. 2**, from centre outwards.

Finishing

Cut binding fabric into 6cm (2¼in) strips. Join into one strip long enough to go round edges of quilt. Fold strip in half lengthwise, wrong sides together, and press to make double binding for extra strength. Pin binding around edges of quilt, right sides together and matching raw edges. Stitch binding to quilt and mitre corners (see page 25). Trim off excess wadding [batting] and lining fabric. Turn binding to wrong side of quilt and hem along stitching line.

Colourwash Crib Quilt

62 × 53cm (24 × 21in)

MATERIALS

Approx 30 × 90cm (12 × 36in) assorted scraps cotton lawn in light-toned colours and prints

Approx 30 × 90cm (12 × 36in) assorted scraps cotton lawn in medium-toned colours and prints

Approx 30 × 90cm (12 × 36in) assorted scraps cotton lawn in dark-toned colours and prints

60 × 90cm (24 × 36in) cotton fabric for lining

60 × 90cm (24 × 36in) white cotton lawn for interlining

20 × 90cm (8 × 36in) cotton fabric for binding

60 × 90cm (24 × 36in) synthetic wadding [batting]

Making the template

Draw a 6.3cm (2½in) square on graph paper. This template includes a 6mm (¼in) seam allowance. Cut out and paste onto thin card [cardboard]. Cut out using a steel ruler and sharp knife.

Preparing the fabric

Using the template, cut out 143 squares from the assorted cotton scraps. Cut about a third of the patches from each group of colours.

Piecing the fabric

Arrange patches on a flat surface in thirteen rows of eleven squares, so that the tones shade down from light to dark (**fig. 1**). With right sides together and taking in 6mm (¼in) seam allowances, join patches first in pairs across each row. Join odd patch to last pair. Press seams open. Replace patches on flat surface in correct position after each seam is sewn and pressed. Then join each pair to the corresponding pair in the row below to make larger squares (**fig. 2**). Press all seams open. Join these larger squares in pairs across each row (**fig. 3**). Proceed in this way until all patches are joined.

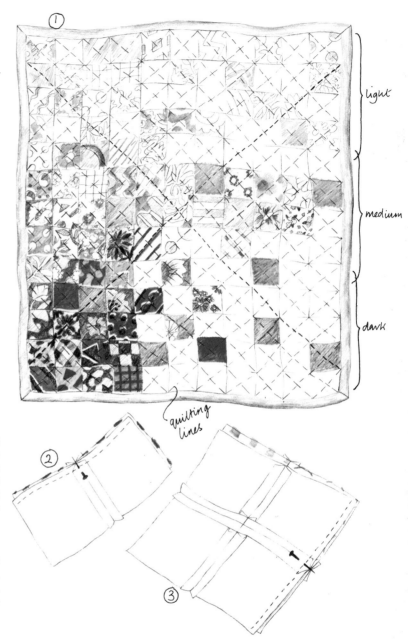

light

medium

dark

quilting lines

Quilting

Measure patchwork and cut lining, wadding [batting] and interlining slightly larger all around. Lay out lining fabric face down on flat surface. Lay wadding [batting] then interlining, on top. Lay patchwork, right side up, on top of interlining. Pin and baste all four layers together, working from centre outwards. Baste firmly around all four sides. Quilt along lines shown in **fig. 1**, working from centre lines outwards. Trim off excess wadding [batting] and lining fabric.

Finishing

Cut binding fabric into 6.5cm (2½in) wide strips. Join strips to make one strip long enough to go round edges of quilt. Fold strip in half lengthwise, wrong sides together, and press to make double binding for extra strength. Pin binding along edges of quilt, right sides together and matching raw edges. Stitch binding to quilt and mitre corners (see page 25). Turn over binding to wrong side of quilt and hem along stitching line.

HEXAGON QUILT
LOG CABIN QUILT

Hexagon Quilt

2.54 × 2.44m (100 × 96in)

MATERIALS

8m × 90cm (9yd × 36in) plain cotton fabric in background colour (O)

50 × 90cm (18 × 36in) printed cotton fabric in each of 3 colours (A, B, F)

1m × 90cm (1yd × 36in) printed cotton fabric in each of 3 colours (E, H, N)

1.20m × 90cm (45 × 36in) printed cotton fabric in each of 5 colours (C, G, J, K, L)

1.85m × 90cm (2yd × 36in) printed cotton fabric in each of 3 colours (D, I, M)

8m × 90cm (9yd × 36in) plain cotton fabric for lining

Making the template

Construct a 2.5cm (1in) sided hexagon (see page 12). Cut it out and paste onto thin card [cardboard]. Cut out using a steel ruler and sharp knife. Alternatively buy ready-made template to same dimensions. Use template to prepare 3564 pattern papers exactly the same size. It is less tedious to make them in batches as you work rather than all at once.

Preparing the fabric

To prepare each hexagonal patch, lay fabric face down on flat surface. Pin pattern paper to fabric. Cut out adding 6mm (¼in) seam allowance all round. Turn over seam allowance onto pattern paper and baste securely through all layers. Prepare the following number of patches in each fabric: A – 64, B – 74, C – 190, D – 266, E – 103, F – 38, G – 184, H – 128, I – 227, J – 177, K – 176, L – 172, M – 295, N – 156, O – 1414.

Piecing the fabric

Join patches (see page 16) beginning at the centre and working outwards. Following layout on page 67, divide bedspread into easily definable pattern areas and build up the design in sections. Join hexagons first in rows and then join

rows. When patchwork is complete, remove all basting threads and pattern papers. Press well on both sides.

Finishing

Turn under edges of patchwork all round and baste. Make up lining fabric to fit, adding 8cm (3in) on all sides. Lay patchwork and lining on flat surface, wrong sides together. Baste the two layers together, working from the centre outwards. Turn under seam allowance on lining fabric and baste. Stitch lining and patchwork together along all four sides with two parallel lines of stitching 3mm (⅛in) apart and as close as possible to the edge. Secure two layers together by quilting lightly around hexagonal shapes at intervals over the quilt.

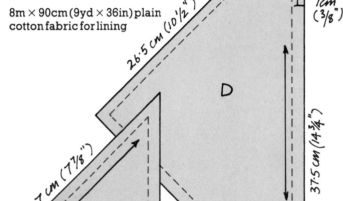

26.5 cm (10½")

19.7 cm (7⅞")

1cm (3/8")

37.5 cm (4¾")

28 cm (11")

18.5 cm (7¼")

8 cm (3/8")

D

C

A

B

①

Arrows indicate grain of fabric

leave 1cm (3/8") seam allowance on two sides and 6mm (¼") on other two sides

Log Cabin Quilt

2.62 × 2.40m (103 × 94in)

MATERIALS

6.5m × 114cm (7yd × 45in) light-coloured lightweight cotton fabric for foundation squares

80 × 90cm (32 × 36in) dark cotton fabric

1.9m × 90cm (2yd × 36in) plain cotton fabric

Approx 12m × 90cm (13yd × 36in) assorted cotton scraps in variety of prints and colours

9m × 90cm (10yd × 36in) cotton fabric for lining

9m × 90cm (10yd × 36in) synthetic wadding [batting]

Making the templates

Copy shapes in **fig. 1** full size on graph paper. Cut out and paste onto thin card [cardboard]. Cut out using a steel ruler and sharp knife. These templates include seam allowances.

Preparing the fabric

Using template A, cut out 199 foundation squares from light cotton fabric. Using template B, cut out 199 squares from dark

cotton fabric. Using template C, cut out 34 small triangles from plain cotton fabric. Using template D, cut out 2 triangles from plain cotton fabric. Cut assorted scraps into strips varying from 2.5cm (1in) to 5cm (2in) wide.

Piecing the fabric

Place a small dark square, right side up, in one corner of a foundation square (**fig. 2**). Pin in

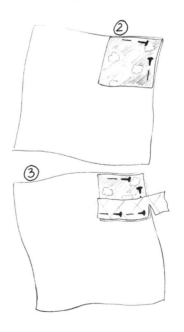

②

③

position. Place one strip, wrong side up, along edge of small square. Pin and cut off surplus strip (**fig. 3**).

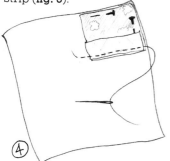

Stitch strip, taking in 6mm (¼in) seam allowance (**fig. 4**).

Open out strip and press (**fig. 5**). Place strip of same width and fabric, wrong side up, across end of first strip.

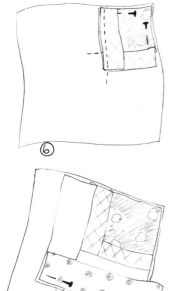

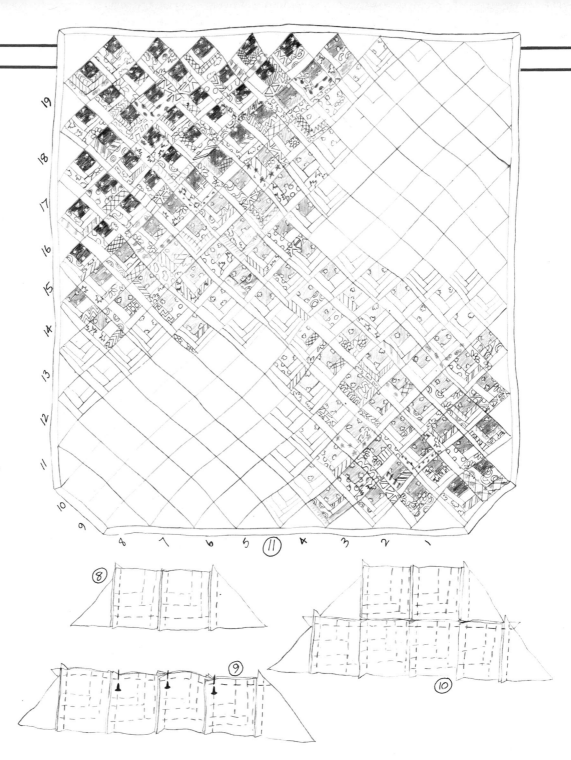

Pin, trim off surplus and stitch as before (**fig. 6**). Open out strip and press. Repeat with strips of varying widths and fabric until foundation square is covered (**fig. 7**). Trim off surplus fabric to edges of foundation square. Make up [finish] remaining foundation squares in the same way.

Following **fig. 8**, join blocks and small triangles in diagonal rows, taking in 1cm (⅜in) seam allowances. Press all seams away from dark squares (**fig. 9**). Join rows, pinning all seams to ensure accurate fit (**fig. 10**) and pressing all seams away from dark squares. Join rows 1–9 together first, then rows 11–19. Finally join row 10 first to one half of patchwork and then the other. Join two large triangles to top corners of patchwork (**fig. 11**). Press seams outwards.

Finishing

Make up [finish] lining fabric and wadding [batting] to fit patchwork. Sandwich wadding [batting] between patchwork and lining, wrong sides together. Pin and baste the three layers together, working from centre outwards. Knot three layers together (see page 25) on seams at intervals all over quilt. Cut remaining plain cotton fabric into 4cm (1½in) wide strips. Join strips together to make one long strip to go round edges of quilt. Pin binding along edges of quilt right sides together and stitch. mitring corners (see page 25). Trim off excess wadding [batting] and lining fabric. Turn over binding to wrong side of quilt, turn under the raw edge and hem along stitching line.

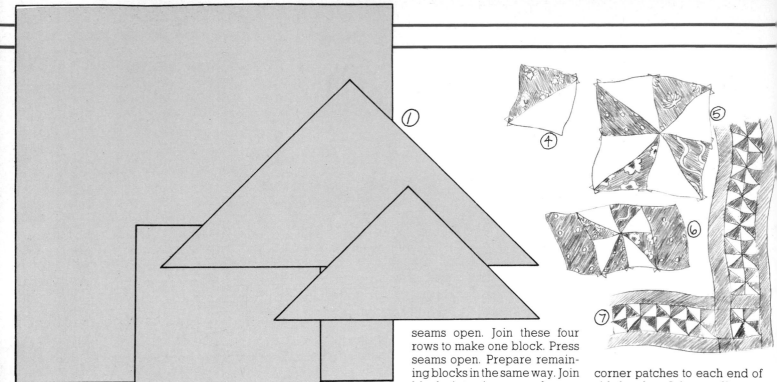

Barcarolle Block Quilt

3.18 × 2.58m (124 × 102in)

MATERIALS

5m × 90cm (5½yd × 36in) dark printed cotton fabric

5m × 90cm (5½yd × 36in) light cotton fabric

Assorted remnants [scraps] printed cotton fabric in variety of colours

9m × 90cm (10yd × 36in) plain cotton fabric for lining

9m × 90cm (10yd × 36in) synthetic wadding [batting]

Making the templates

Trace shapes in **fig. 1**. Cut out and paste onto thin card [cardboard]. Cut out using a steel ruler and sharp knife.

Preparing the fabric

The quilt is made up of sixty-three blocks. For each one you will need sixteen small triangles in dark fabric, eight large triangles in light fabric and four large and four small squares in a variety of colours. Cut out shapes, adding 6mm (¼in) seam allowances all round each one. For the border, cut out 272 large triangles in light

fabric and 272 large triangles in dark fabric. Cut remaining dark fabric into 6cm (2½in) wide strips.

Piecing the fabric

Taking in 6mm (¼in) seam allowances, join small triangles to large triangles (**fig. 2**). Press seams open. Join these patches to large and small squares in rows as shown in **fig. 3**. Press

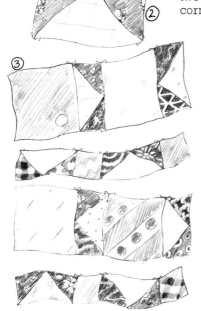

seams open. Join these four rows to make one block. Press seams open. Prepare remaining blocks in the same way. Join blocks into nine rows of seven blocks each. Join rows, pinning seams carefully to ensure accurate fit. For the border, join dark and light triangles together in pairs to form squares (**fig. 4**). Join these squares in fours to create a windmill effect (**fig. 5**). Join fifteen windmills together in a long strip for top border and fifteen for bottom border. Join nineteen windmills in a long strip for each side, leaving four for the corners. Join the 6cm (2½in) wide strips of dark fabric together to make four strips 211cm (83in) long, four strips 271cm (108in) long and eight strips 15cm (6in) long. Join one 15cm (6in) strip to two opposite sides of each corner square (**fig. 6**). Join

corner patches to each end of side borders. Join one of longer strips to each side of each side border and one of shorter strips to each side of top and bottom borders. Join top and bottom borders to patchwork. Join side borders (**fig. 7**). Press all seams open.

Quilting and finishing

Lay patchwork face down on flat surface. Lay wadding [batting] on top to within 13mm (½in) of edges, cutting it to fit. Baste the two layers together. Make up the lining fabric to fit. With right sides together, seam lining to quilt along three sides. Turn right side out and slipstitch along remaining side. Quilt by hand or machine along lines shown in **fig. 8**.

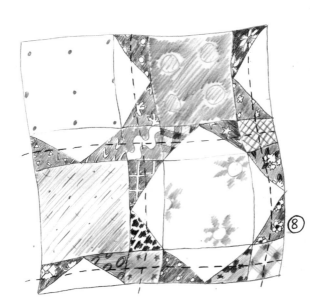

Interlocking Block Quilt

2.97 × 2.49m (116 × 98in)

MATERIALS

6m × 90cm (6½yd × 36in) assorted remnants [scraps] in dark printed cotton fabric

6m × 90cm (6½yd × 36in) assorted remnants in light printed cotton fabric

9m × 90cm (10yd × 36in) cotton fabric for lining

9m × 90cm (10yd × 36in) synthetic wadding [batting]

Making the templates

For main block templates, trace shapes in **fig. 1**. Cut out and paste onto thin card [cardboard]. Cut out using a steel ruler and sharp knife. Make border template (**fig. 2**) in the same way.

Preparing the fabric

The quilt is made up of ninety-nine blocks. For each one you will need sixteen patches, four cut from each main block template. For twenty-five blocks, cut all patches from light fabric; for twenty-four blocks, cut all patches from dark fabric. For the remaining fifty blocks, cut half the patches (two from each template shape) from dark and half from light fabric. Prepare patches for border when main body of quilt is finished to enable you to estimate correct number of patches needed. Border patches are cut from a mixture of light and dark fabric. Cut out all shapes adding 6mm (¼in) seam allowances around each one.

Piecing the fabric

Join mixed colour blocks following layout in **fig. 3**. Start with centre squares and work outwards. At each stage press seams towards dark patches. Piece remaining blocks in the same way, using either all dark or all light patches. Make twenty-five light blocks and twenty-four dark blocks. Join blocks to make eleven rows of nine blocks, alternating dark and light blocks as shown (**fig.**

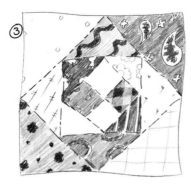

4). Join rows, pinning seams to ensure accurate fit. Join border triangles to make strip long enough to go round patchwork. Cut remaining dark fabric into 6cm (2½in) wide strips and join to make two strips long enough to edge strip of triangles on both sides (**fig. 5**). Join border to main patchwork piece, mitring corners.

Quilting and finishing

Lay patchwork face down on flat surface. Measure quilt and make up wadding [batting] and lining to fit. Lay wadding [batting] on top of quilt and trim to within 13mm (½in) of edges all round. Baste these two layers together. With right sides together, seam lining to quilt along three sides. Turn right side out and slipstitch along remaining side. Catchstitch at intervals through all three layers to prevent wadding [batting] slipping when in use.

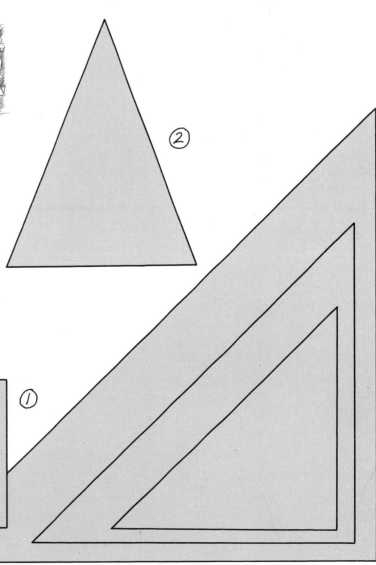

WALL HANGING

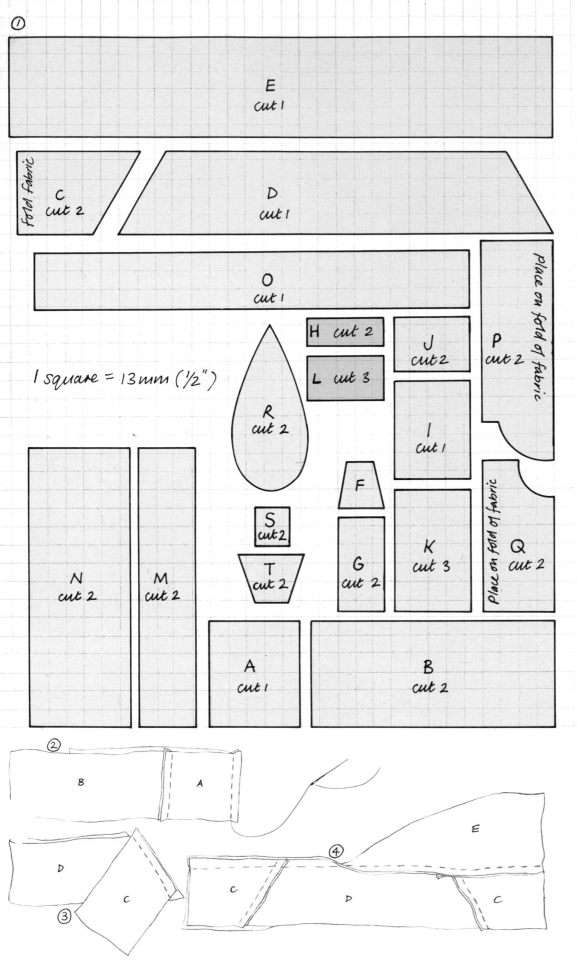

Wall Hanging

51 × 51cm (20 × 20in)

MATERIALS

10 × 90cm (4 × 36in) cotton fabric for sky

8 × 35cm (3 × 14in) cotton fabric for roof

10 × 90cm (4 × 36in) cotton fabric for house walls and chimney stacks

15 × 90cm (6 × 36in) cotton fabric for garden walls and chimney pots

10 × 40cm (4 × 16in) cotton fabric for windows

10 × 40cm (4 × 16in) cotton fabric for garden

10cm (4in) square cotton fabric for path

10cm (4in) square cotton fabric for door

15cm (6in) square cotton fabric for trees

5 × 90cm (2 × 36in) cotton fabric for window sills and other decorative features

Assorted scraps cotton fabric for tree trunks, tubs and step

30 × 90cm (12 × 36in) cotton fabric for border

30 × 90cm (12 × 36in) cotton fabric for binding, narrow border and loops

60cm (24in) square cotton fabric for backing

60cm (24in) square synthetic wadding [batting]

55cm (22in) long bamboo or dowelling

Making the templates
Copy shapes in **fig. 1** full size on graph paper. Cut out and paste onto thin card [cardboard]. Cut out using a steel ruler and sharp knife. Label templates as shown. Shapes F, G, R, S, T are appliqué templates. The rest are patchwork templates.

Preparing the fabric
Cut out the required number of shapes in the appropriate fabrics. Cut window sill fabric lengthwise into 2cm (¾in) wide strips.

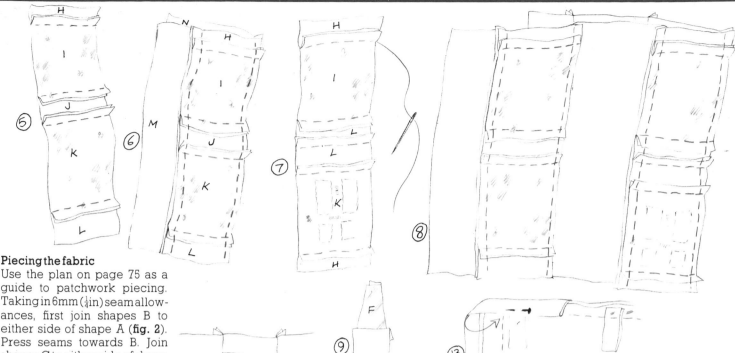

Piecing the fabric

Use the plan on page 75 as a guide to patchwork piecing. Taking in 6mm ($\frac{1}{4}$in) seam allowances, first join shapes B to either side of shape A (**fig. 2**). Press seams towards B. Join shapes C to either side of shape D (**fig. 3**). Press seams towards D. Join E to this strip (**fig. 4**). Press seams towards D. Join shapes H, I, J, K and L together (**fig. 5**) to make two side window panels. Press seams towards wall. Join M and N to either side of each window panel (**fig. 6**). Press seams towards wall. Join shapes H, I, L, L, K and H together to make centre door panel (**fig. 7**). Press seams towards walls. Join side window panels to either side of door panel (**fig. 8**). Press seams towards walls. Join shape O to the top of this panel. Press seam towards O. Clip curved edges of garden walls and turn them under. Pin and baste onto sky shapes P. Hem in place. Join these strips to either side of house. Press seams towards house. Join roof panel to house. Press seam towards house. Join garden panel to bottom of house. Press towards garden.

Appliqué

Turn under raw edges of window sill strips lengthwise. Baste and press. Turn under side edges of chimney pots and stacks. Baste and press. Join pots and stacks (**fig. 9**). Turn under bottom edges of stacks. Place stacks in position at each corner of roof, lining tops of pots with top of sky. Hem in position. Cut two 4.5cm (1$\frac{3}{4}$in) long pieces off window sill strip. Turn under raw edges.

Hem in place along tops of stacks. In the same way, appliqué one 6.5cm (2$\frac{1}{2}$in) strip to window sill at the bottom of each window. Appliqué one 11cm (4$\frac{1}{2}$in) window sill strip at each side of door, one 7.5cm (3in) strip above door and one 7.5cm (3in) strip above fanlight (**fig. 10**). Appliqué one 30.5cm (12in) strip either side of shape O (**fig. 11**). Clip round curved bases of trees and turn edges under. Baste and press. Turn under side edges of trunks and all sides of tubs. Join trees, trunks and tubs and hem in position either side of door. Embroider panels, number, letter box, handle and knocker on door as desired (**fig. 12**).

Borders

For narrow border, cut out 2.5cm (1in) wide strips, two 37cm (14$\frac{1}{2}$in) long and two 39cm (15$\frac{1}{2}$in) long. Join two short strips to top and bottom of picture. Join two long strips either side. Press seams towards borders. For wide borders, cut out 7.5cm (3in) wide strips, two 39cm (15$\frac{1}{2}$in) long and two 52cm (20$\frac{1}{2}$in) long. Join two short borders to top and bottom of picture and two long borders to each side, pressing all seams outwards.

Quilting

Sandwich wadding [batting] between backing fabric and picture, wrong sides together. Pin and baste all three layers together, working from centre outwards. Baste firmly around edges. Machine or hand quilt around all shapes, working from centre outwards.

Finishing

Cut out a strip of fabric 4cm (1$\frac{1}{2}$in) wide and 56cm (22in) long for loops. Fold strip in half, right sides together. Stitch edges, taking in 6mm ($\frac{1}{4}$in) seam allowance to make tube. Turn tube right side out and press. Cut into seven 8cm (3in) lengths. Fold each one in half. Cut binding fabric into 6cm (2$\frac{1}{4}$in) wide strips. Join into one strip long enough to go round edges of wall hanging. Fold in half lengthwise, wrong sides together, and press. Pin binding round wall hanging, right sides together, and matching raw edges. Stitch down and mitre corners (see page 25). Trim off excess wadding [batting] and backing fabric. Position seven loops at intervals along top of picture on wrong side. Hand sew in position (**fig. 13**). Turn binding over to wrong side and hem along stitching line. Thread bamboo or dowelling through loops.

Patchwork Suppliers

UNITED KINGDOM
A wide selection of fabrics and sewing accessories are available from the following:

John Lewis & Co Ltd
Oxford Street
London W1A 1EX
Tel: 01 629 7711

McCullock & Wallis Ltd
25–26 Dering Street
London W1R 0BH
Tel: 01 629 0311

Mace & Nairn
89 Crane Street
Salisbury
Wiltshire
Tel: Salisbury 6903

Christine Riley
53 Barclay Street
Stonehaven
Kincardineshire AB3 2AR
Tel: Stonehaven 3228

The following sell patchwork supplies by mail order:

Strawberry Fayre
Stockbridge
Hants SO20 6HF

fine American cotton fabrics, waddings, hoops and threads (send s.a.e. for details)

The Patchwork Dog and the Calico Cat
21 Chalk Farm Road
London NW1

fabrics, waddings, hoops and threads (send s.a.e. for details)

The Quiltery
Tacolneston
Norwich
Norfolk
NR16 1DW

templates (send s.a.e. for details)

The Handicraft Shop
5 Oxford Road
Altrincham
Cheshire

threads and templates (send s.a.e. for details)

Stitches
30a St Leonard's Road
Windsor
Berkshire

cotton fabrics and templates (send s.a.e. for details)

The Silver Thimble
33 Gay Street
Bath
Avon BA1 2NT

templates (send s.a.e. for details)

Mrs J M Keane
Hazel Barton,
Medstead Alton,
Hants

selected cotton fabrics (send s.a.e. for details)

UNITED STATES
The following nationwide chain stores usually stock a wide selection of patchwork supplies: **Ben Franklin Stores; Jefferson Stores; Kay Mart; M H Lamston; The May Co; Neisners; J C Penney Stores; Sears Roebuck; Two Guys** and **Woolworth's.**

The following sell patchwork supplies by mail order:

American Handicrafts
2617 W Seventh Street
Fort Worth, Texas 76707

all craft supplies

The Counting House at the Hammock Shop
Box 155
Pawleys Island,
So Carolina 29585

materials, threads, hoops needles, frames

Economy Handicrafts
50–21 69th Street
Woodside, New York 11377

all craft supplies

Lee Wards
Elgin, Illinois 60120

all craft supplies

Peters Valley Craftsmen
Layton, New Jersey 07851

all craft supplies

The Stearns & Foster Co
PO Box 15380
Cincinnati, Ohio 45215

batting and frames

Vermont County Store
Weston, Vermont 05161

calico prints

INDEX

Acknowledgments

The publishers are very grateful to the following for kindly lending work to be photographed:

Carol Swatton: shower cap 35; neck purse, cosmetic bag, holdall 38.
Brenda Durling: cathedral window purse and cushions 42.
Carol Robinson: occasional bag 43.
Gisela Banbury: sewing case 46.
Hazel Wittal of Quad Quilts: pincushion 46.
Deirdre Amsden: star and square cushion covers 50; alphabet cot quilt 58; houses cot quilt 62; colourwash crib quilt 63; log cabin quilt 66; wall hanging 74.
Pauline Burbidge: fruit basket cushion cover 54.
Michele Walker: Michele's quilt 54.
Margaret Brandebourg: interlocking quilt, barcarolle quilt 70.

The publishers would also like to thank **Ron Simpson** and **Paul Taylor** for their kind permission to reproduce the photographs on pages 14, 26 left, and 33 above.

The publishers would also like to thank the following organisations for the loan of items used in photography:

pages 50–51: **New Dimension**, Ipswich, Suffolk (furniture).
pages 62–63: **Graham and Green**, 7 Elgin Crescent, London W11 (cot pillows); **Warners** (lace curtains).
pages 70–71: **Graham and Green** (artificial flowers).
pages 74–75: **Warners** (furnishing fabric).

Photography by: **American Museum** 8, 9, 28 left and above right, 29 above left and right, 30, 31 below, 33 left; **Theo Bergstrom** Endpapers; **Oliver Hatch** 14, 26 left, 43 above; **Kilkenny Design Workshops** 26 right, 27, 38 below right, 29 below, 31 above, 33 below right; **Sandra Lousada** 38–9, 58–9; **Spike Powell** 4–5, 42–3, 50–1, 62–3, 63, 66, 66–7, 70–1, 74–5; **Peter Rauter** 10–11, 34–5, 46–7, 47, 54–5; **Scala** 6; **Welsh Folk Museum** 7.

Illustrations by **Lucy Su**

Photographic styling by **Margaret Colvin** and **Sonia Fancett**

The publishers are particularly grateful to **Liberty of London Prints Ltd** of Regent Street, London, for their kind permission to reproduce their fabrics in this book. Liberty fabrics are shown on the cover and endpapers and are used in the patchwork designs on the following pages: title page (log cabin quilt); page 10; page 19 (pincushion); page 35; pages 38-39; pages 42-43; pages 46-47 (pincushions); pages 50-51; pages 62-63; pages 66-67 (log cabin quilt); pages 74-75.